W9-BHV-103

THE ULTIMATE BOOK OF THE

OF THE

p

This is a Parragon Publishing Book
This edition published in 2001

Parragon Publishing
Queen Street House
4 Queen Street
Bath BA11HE, UK

Produced by Miles Kelly Publishing Ltd
Bardfield Centre, Great Bardfield, Essex CM7 4SL

Authors
Keith Lye
&Philip Steele

Cover Design
David West Children's Book

British Library Cataloguing-in-Pubblication Data

A catalogue record for this book is available from the British Library.

ISBN 0-75256-390-4

Printed in Italy

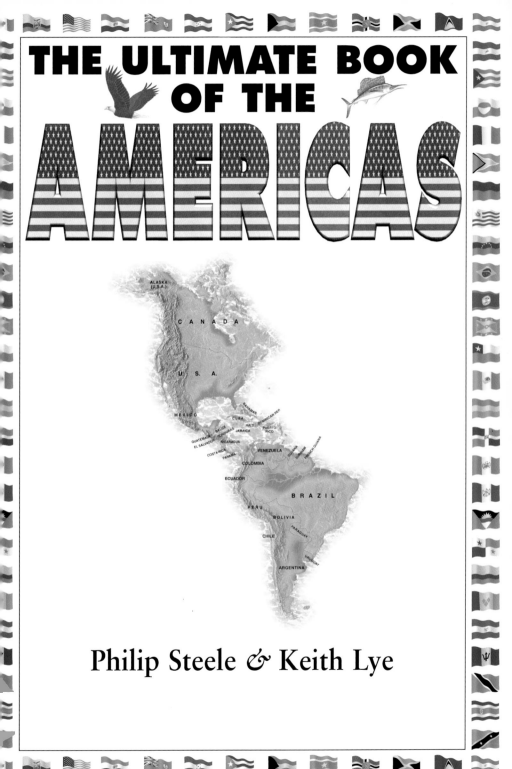

THE ULTIMATE BOOK
OF THE
AMERICAS

Philip Steele & Keith Lye

CONTENTS

THE AMERICAS
10

CANADA AND GREENLAND
CANADA • GREENLAND • ST PIERRE AND MIQUELON
12

UNITED STATES OF AMERICA
UNITED STATES OF AMERICA • BERMUDA
18

MEXICO AND CENTRAL AMERICA
BELIZE • COSTA RICA • EL SALVADOR • GUATEMALA • HONDURAS •
MEXICO • NICARAGUA • PANAMA
28

THE AMERICAS

North and South America are two great continents, lying between the Atlantic and Pacific Oceans. They are joined together by Central America, which narrows to a strip of land called the Isthmus of Panama. This is cut in two by the Panama Canal, which links the two oceans. Tropical Central America is bordered to the east by the Caribbean Sea, which is enclosed by the islands of the Greater and Lesser Antilles.

▲ Cactus

North America is dominated by a mountain system called the Rockies, which stretches from north to south. In the far north, frozen tundra yields to forest. To the south lie the prairies – rolling glasslands which are now used for grazing or crops, parts of a great plain drained by the Mississippi-Missouri river system. In the southern United States and Central America are rocky canyons, wetlands, volcanoes and deserts.

In South America, the Rockies are matched by mighty Andes mountain chain. To the east, a maze of waterways flows into the river Amazon, which is surrounded by the world's largest tropical rainforests. South American grasslands include the Llanos of Venezuela and the Argentinean Pampa. There are windy plateaus and coastal deserts. The continent ends in the bleak island of Tierra ael Fuego, which reaches out like a claw towards Antarctica.

◀ Boatbuilder, Barbados

▼ Lake Moraine, Canada

◀ Sailfish

◀ Toltec temple, Mexico

N A D A

S . A

BAHAMAS

CUBA

DOMINICAN REP.

HAITI

BELIZE

GUATEMALA

HONDURAS

JAMAICA

PUERTO RICO

SALVADOR

NICARAGUA

COSTA RICA

PANAMA

VENEZUELA

GUYANA

SURINAM

FRENCH GUIANA

COLOMBIA

EDUADOR

B R A Z I L

PERU

BOLIVIA

PARAGUAY

CHILE

URUGUAY

ARGENTINA

▲ Disneyworld, United States of America

◀ Panama hat

▲ Harley Davidson
Electra Glide, 1988

▼ Waterside
house, Belize

▲ CN Tower,
Toronto, Canada

▼ Alaska

11

Canada and Greenland

▲ **Land of ice**
Icy mountains rise above a sea inlet near Anagfallik, Greenland. All human settlement is around the coast.

Greenland is the world's biggest island. In fact, it is really several islands, which are welded together by a cap of permanent ice. This is up to 9,840 feet deep in places. Icebergs break off from its glaciers and float out to sea. Only one-sixth of Greenland is ice-free.

▼ **Tundra life**
The Arctic tundra supports a wide range of wildlife, including birds, such as the ptarmigan, and the caribou, a North American reindeer.

Across the Davis Strait lies Canada, by area the world's second largest nation. Its islands are scattered like pieces of a jigsaw puzzle across the Arctic, between the Beaufort and Labrador Seas. The tundra, a wide expanse of ice and snow, remains frozen all year round. However during the brief summer, the snow melts and lies in pools which attract insects and migrating birds.

Most of the Canadian mainland is taken up by a broad belt of forests and glacial lakes. A vast slab of ancient rock, the Canadian Shield, borders Hudson Bay. In the west are the high peaks of the Mackenzie, Rocky and Coast ranges, which descend to the moist, green coast of British Columbia.

The southern border with the United States crosses the prairies and the Great Lakes. The St Lawrence River and Seaway link Lake Ontario with the Atlantic Ocean. Here, the warm Gulf Stream meets the cold Labrador Current, bringing fog to the waters off Newfoundland, Canada's Maritime provinces and the little French islands of St Pierre and Miquelon.

▲ **In the Rockies**
Moraine Lake may be visited in the Banff National Park, in Alberta. Its vivid blue color is caused by a silt known as 'rock flour.'

FACTS

CANADA
Area: 3,849,652 sq miles
Population: 30.0 million
Capital: Ottawa
Other cities: Toronto, Montréal, Vancouver
Highest point: Mount Logan (19,524 ft)
Official languages: English, French
Currency: Canadian dollar

GREENLAND
Kalaallit Nunaat – Grønland
SELF-GOVERNING ISLAND TERRITORY OF DENMARK
Area: 839,999 sq miles
Population: 0.06 million
Capital: Nuuk (Godthåb)
Highest point: Gunnbjørn Fjeld (12,138 ft)
Official languages: Danish, Greenlandic (Kalaallisut)
Currency: Danish krone

ST PIERRE AND MIQUELON
TERRITORIAL COLLECTIVITY OF FRANCE
Area: 93 sq miles
Population: 6,500
Capital: Saint-Pierre
Official language: French
Currency: French franc

▶ The beaver
Beavers live on many Canadian lakes. They use their powerful gnawing teeth to fell trees and shred wood.

▶ Tundra soil
A pingo is a mound of soil filled with a core of expanding ice. When the ice melts, the pingo collapses.

GREENLAND

N
W   E
S

CANADA

LINCOLN SEA

ARCTIC OCEAN

Ellesmere Island

Denmark Strait

G R E E N L A N D

Melville Island

Devon Island

BAFFIN BAY

Banks Island

Prince of Wales Island

BEAUFORT SEA

Victoria Island

Baffin Island

Davis Strait

Dawson

Norman Wells

Great Bear Lake

FOXE BASIN

LABRADOR SEA

ASKA (U.S.A.)

YUKON TERRITORY

Whitehorse

Mt Logan 5,951 m

MACKENZIE MOUNTAINS

NORTHWEST TERRITORIES

Dubawnt Lake

Southampton Island

Hudson Strait

HORN MOUNTAINS

Yellowknife

Great Slave Lake

Fort Resolution

Coats Island

Mansel Island

Ungava Peninsula

HUDSON BAY

Fort Smith

Liard

CARIBOU MOUNTAINS

Lake Athabasca

Churchill

Feuilles

Goose Bay

BRITISH COLUMBIA

Peace River

CANADA

Reindeer Lake

Belcher Islands

La Grande Rivière

NEWFOUNDLAND

Rupert

Peace

ALBERTA

Nelson

Churchill

JAMES BAY

OTISH MOUNTAINS

Gander

Newfoundland

St John's

Prince George

Edmonton

MANITOBA

Akimiski Island

Anticosti Island

 Kamloops

N. Saskatchewan

Red Deer

Prince Albert

Lake Winnipeg

Albany

Péribonca

Gulf of St. Lawrence

PRINCE EDWARD ISLAND

Vancouver Island

Vancouver

Calgary

Medicine Hat

Saskatoon

SASKATCHEWAN

Winnipegosis

ONTARIO

QUEBEC

St. Lawrence

NEW BRUNSWICK

Charlottetown

NOVA SCOTIA

Victoria

S. Saskatchewan

Regina

Lake Manitoba

Winnipeg

Lake Nipigon

Quebec

Fredericton

St John

Halifax

U N I T E D   S T A T E S   O F   A M E R I C A

Thunder Bay

Montreal

ATLANTIC OCEAN

Lake Superior

Georgian Bay

Ottawa

Lake Huron

Toronto

Lake Ontario

Hamilton

Niagara Falls

Windsor

Lake Erie

◀ Takkakaw Falls
Takkakaw means 'wonderful' in the language of the Cree people. The falls tumble over a drop of 833 feet in the Yoho National Park, British Columbia.

▶ Bath time!
The moose can stand 7.55 feet at the shoulder. This one is pictured at Pukaskawa National Park, Ontario, on the north shore of Lake Superior.

◀ Musk ox

13

Canada and Greenland

GREENLAND IS A DEPENDENCY OF DENMARK, but has been self-governing since 1981. With the exception of Antarctica, it is the world's least-populated land. Temperatures on the central ice cap can drop below –85°F, but ocean currents keep the southwest coast relatively mild. The fishing industry is a major employer.

In Canada, too, the severe climate of the north has restricted settlement. Seventy-seven percent of Canadians are town-dwellers and the big cities are all in the south, where the climate is milder and transport easier. The Canadian capital is Ottawa, a city in southeastern Ontario. The commercial centers are the much larger cities of Toronto and Montréal.

Canada is an independent nation whose head of state is the British monarch. It is organized on federal lines, with provinces and territories. Canada was a founder member in 1994 of the North American Free Trade Agreement (NAFTA), which strengthened economic ties with the

▲ In search of cod
The Grand Banks are shallow waters off the coast of Newfoundland. They have attracted international fishing fleets for about five centuries, but stocks of cod have declined in recent years.

▲ Sky level
Toronto's CN Tower, over 1,815 feet high, is the world's tallest structure. Its viewing platform is a dizzying 1,444 feet above the ground.

▼ Lumberjack years
The loggers who felled the Canadian forests a century ago had few mechanical aids. They lived hard lives in remote camps.

◄ Fighting the blaze
A helicopter moves in to fight a forest fire. Canada's vast conifer forests stretch in a broad belt across central and northern regions, from British Columbia to the Laurentian Plateau.

▶ Logging today
Canada has over 1132.5 million acres of forest and is the world's leading exporter of forest products. These include timber in various forms, wood pulp and paper.

◀ Toronto skyline
With a population of nearly five million, Toronto is Canada's biggest city. It is a national center of business and communications.

◀ Space tech
Canada has an important aerospace industry. It built this robotic lifting device, called the Canadarm, for use on American Space Shuttles.

▼ Oil rig, Alberta
Over 90 percent of Canada's reserves of oil and natural gas are found in Alberta province. Major production regions are at Lloydminster, Fort McMurray and here, at Cold Lake.

United States and Mexico to the south.

The Canadian prairies supply wheat to the world and provide pasture for cattle. The great forests send timber to the sawmills. There are reserves of oil, natural gas, copper, gold, iron ore and nickel, and there are plenty of rivers and lakes to provide hydroelectric power. Factories manufacture cars, paper, steel and chemicals.

Food products include maple syrup, apples, cheese and beer. Until recently Newfoundland lay off one of the richest fishing grounds in the world, but overfishing has led to dwindling stocks and a ban on trawling until numbers recover.

Like the United States, Canada is a melting pot of peoples and cultures. For the last 30 years Canadian politics have been dominated by the future of Québec province, where a large number of French-speakers wish to break away from the rest of Canada altogether. English-speaking Canadians share many of the interests of their American neighbors – but are always keen to emphasise their own independent way of life.

▲ In Montréal
Montréal, capital of Québec province, is the chief city of French-speaking Canada and a center of commerce and the arts. Shop signs are often in French.

▲ ▶ Sugar maple
Maple syrup is boiled up from a sweet sap, collected from the maple tree. It was invented long ago, by native peoples of the St Lawrence valley. Today it is popular in Canada and the United States, where it is poured over pancakes and waffles.

15

Canada and Greenland

THE FIRST PEOPLE TO SETTLE Canada were prehistoric peoples from the Asian region of Siberia. Their descendants include the First Peoples who live in Canada today – groups such as the Mohawk, Micmac, Innu, Cree, Dene and Kwakiutl.

▲ **Across the Arctic**
Vehicles fitted with skis, such as snow mobiles, have become the most popular method of travel for the Inuit and other peoples of the north.

They were followed by waves of Inuit hunters, who set up scattered settlements across the Canadian Arctic and Greenland. Except in Greenland, the descendants of all these native peoples are today greatly outnumbered by later immigrants. They have faced a long struggle to gain rights to their own land, but there have been successes, too. A huge but very sparsely-populated area of Canada became the Inuit territory of Nunavut in 1999.

Vikings from Scandinavia arrived in Canada and Greenland about 1,000 years ago. They soon lost their foothold in Canada, but stayed in Greenland for about 500 years. Danish traders returned to Greenland in the 1700s and it later became a Danish colony.

▲ **Erik Cove, Québec, 1904**
A hundred years ago, hunting met all the Inuits' needs, providing meat, hide and fur for clothing, bones for needles and gut for thread.

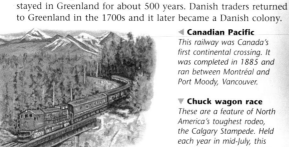

◄ **Canadian Pacific**
This railway was Canada's first continental crossing. It was completed in 1885 and ran between Montréal and Port Moody, Vancouver.

▼ **Chuck wagon race**
These are a feature of North America's toughest rodeo, the Calgary Stampede. Held each year in mid-July, this celebration of cowboy skills dates back to 1912.

► **Totem poles**
Tall poles carved from cedarwood were erected in villages of Canada's Pacific coast by native chiefs. They represented guardian spirits and histories of the family or tribe.

▼ Monster mash
In a different kind of stampede, heavy-metal racers with big tires show off in Calgary, Alberta.

▼ The champions
Ice hockey was first played in Canada in the 1850s and today is the country's most popular sport.

▷ Winterlude
The Winterlude festival is held each February in Ottawa. Events include sculpture in ice and snow, and skating on the Rideau Canal.

It was the French who explored and colonised the lands around Canada's St Lawrence River in the 1500s, while the British went on to trade around Hudson Bay. In the 1700s the two nations fought bitterly for control of Canada. The British won. Their numbers grew after the 1770s, as families loyal to Britain fled northwards from the newly independent United States.

The French retained their language and their Roman Catholic faith, but by 1867 Canada was united as a dominion within the British empire. Many more peoples settled in Canada as the nation expanded across the prairies towards British Columbia. Newfoundland and Labrador joined Canada in 1948.

Although people of British (especially Scots) and French descent still make up a large percentage of the Canadian population, it has grown in the last two centuries to include Ukrainians, Dutch, Russians, Poles, Germans, Italians, Chinese, Indians, Vietnamese and Afro-Caribbeans.

◁ Newfoundlanders
Fishing is a way of life on the remote island of Newfoundland, off the Atlantic coast. The islanders voted to join Canada in 1949.

▷ Dogsled, Québec
Teams of dogs pulled sleds in the old Arctic and are still used today. Dogsled racing is a popular sport.

◁ The 'Mounties'
The Northwest Mounted Police, with their red coats and distinctive hats, were founded in 1873. They tamed the Wild West. In 1920 they became a national force, the Royal Canadian Mounted Police.

TIMELINE

AD	
900s	Vikings discover and settle Greenland
1410	Greenland colonists lose contact with Scandinavia
1497	John Cabot discovers Newfoundland
1534	Jacques Cartier explores St Lawrence River
1608	Samuel de Champlain founds Québec
1642	Montréal founded
1670	Hudson's Bay Company established
1713	British gain Newfoundland
1759	British defeat French at Québec
1763	Canada becomes a British colony
1776	Founding of KGH, the Royal Greenland Trading Company
1814	Greenland becomes Danish colony
1840	Act of Union joins Upper and Lower Canada
1867	Dominion of Canada: Ontario, Québec, Nova Scotia, New Brunswick
1870s	Manitoba, British Columbia, Prince Edward Island join Canada
1896	Klondike gold rush (until 1898)
1905	Alberta, Saskatchewan join Canada
1914	World War I (until 1918): Canada joins Allies
1939	World War II (until 1945): Canada joins Allies
1949	Newfoundland joins Canada
1959	St Lawrence Seaway opened
1968	Separatists demand free Québec
1979	Home rule for Greenland
1994	Canada in North American Free Trade Agreement (NAFTA)
1995	Québec referendum rejects separatism
1999	Self-governing homeland for Inuit (Nunavut)

United States of America

▲ Maize

Central North America is dominated by the United States of America (USA). The only other territory is a group of 150 small islands, lying 696 miles to the southeast of the state of New York, in the North Atlantic Ocean. These make up a British colony called Bermuda.

Forty-eight of the United States lie between the Canadian and Mexican borders. This is the American heartland, with coastlines on both the North Atlantic and North Pacific oceans. It is a land of amazing variety, where long, lonely highways cut through deserts and mountains, farmland and forest, linking together the big cities of the east and west.

To the north, beyond Canadian territory, lies Alaska. This includes great areas of Arctic wilderness, forming the largest state of all. Its islands are inhabited by large grizzly bears and its waters by schools of whales.

▲ **Niagara Falls**
These spectacular waterfalls are on the United States-Canada border. Not only a tourist attraction, they are also a major source of hydroelectric power.

▲ **Bald eagle**

▲ **Liberty**
This 302-feet high statue guards New York City's harbor. A gift from the French, it was dedicated in 1886.

Far to the west, the volcanic Hawaiian islands form a Pacific outpost of the USA. Tourists come here to enjoy the warm climate and to see the island's spectacular volcanoes.

The area of the United States as a whole makes it the fourth largest country in the world, after the Russian Federation, Canada and China.

◀ **Bryce Canyon**
Pink, orange and buff-colored rocks have been eroded by wind, water and ice into extraordinary pinnacles at this national park, in Utah.

FACTS

UNITED STATES OF AMERICA
Area: 3,615,255 sq miles
Population: 265.3 million
Capital: Washington DC
Other cities: New York City, Los Angeles, Chicago
Highest point: Mt McKinley (20,321 feet)
Official language: English
Currency: US dollar

BERMUDA
British Overseas Territory
Area: 20.5 sq miles
Population: 0.06 million
Capital: Hamilton
Official language: English
Currency: Bermuda dollar

▲ **Chipmunk**

Alaska

▲ **The largest state**
*Alaska is a land of misty
shores, islands, towering
mountains, glaciers and
remote, snowy wilderness.*

**UNITED STATES
OF AMERICA**

N W E S

▼ **Organ Pipe Cactus
National Monument**
*Summer temperatures can soar to
105.8°C in this part of Arizona. Spiny
cacti, bearing pink flowers in summer,
line the Ajo Mountain drive.*

BERMUDA

Hawaiian islands

▲ **Sea cow**
*The rare manatee
is found along the
Florida coast.*

19

United States of America

THE NORTHEASTERN UNITED STATES IS A temperate land of green river valleys, woodland and rocky shores. The coastal plain is narrow in the north but widens to the south of Chesapeake Bay, where it is fringed by long, sandy beaches. The flat lands rise to the Appalachian system, which includes the Green, White, Allegheny and Blue mountain ranges. In the far southeast, the sunny peninsula of Florida ends in a string of small sandy islands, known as keys. Here, the calm can be shattered by savage hurricanes.

To the south of the Great Lakes lies a broad plain, drained by the Missouri and Mississippi rivers. The latter forms a muddy delta where it enters the steamy Gulf of Mexico. Flat, dusty farmland stretches westwards, bedevilled by whirlwinds called tornadoes. The American prairies, once a great sea of grass stretching to the badlands at the foot of the Rocky Mountains, are now patchworked with fields of crops, farm buildings and ranches.

▲ **The Everglades**
The Everglades is a vast system of wetlands which drains southern Florida. It is home to alligators, tree snails and egrets.

▼ **Okefenokee swamp**
This wildlife refuge lies on the Georgia-Florida border. It is a maze of waterways, marshes and floating islands. Its bald cypress trees are draped with Spanish moss.

▲ **The colors of fall**
New England – the far northeastern region of the United States – is famous for the beautiful reds, oranges and browns of its temperate woodlands, before the leaves fall in autumn.

▲ **The Colorado Rockies**
The Rocky Mountains National Park is entered from the town of Estes Park, Colorado, on the Big Thompson River. The massive ranges of the Rockies form the backbone of the North American continent.

Golden Gate Bridge
*This is California's most
famous landmark.
Opened in 1937,
the bridge crosses
a strait which
connects San
Francisco Bay
with the open
Pacific Ocean.*

Sea lions
*Graceful in the
water, comical on
land, sea lions
live on many
islands off the
Californian coast.
Males can be up to
9.84 feet long.*

Fire warning
*A notice in Bryce Canyon,
Utah, warns of the
danger of forest fires.
America's vast forests
are often devastated
by terrifying blazes.*

Grand Canyon
*In Arizona, the Colorado
River has carved out the
world's biggest gorge.
In parts, it plunges to a
depth of 0.93 miles.*

Beyond the massive peaks of the Rockies lie dazzling salt flats and rocks worn into bizarre shapes by the wind and weather. It was the Colorado River which cut out the world's most impressive gorge, the Grand Canyon. The deserts of the southwest shimmer in the heat.

The Coast, Cascade and Sierra Nevada ranges of the far west act as a barrier to rain-bearing winds from the ocean. However the western slopes catch the rain, making the forests of the northwest cool, moist and green. The north of California has a pleasant, spring-like climate when not shrouded in fog. The south is hotter and drier.

Night-raider
*The raccoon, with its
banded eyes and tail, often
raids dustbins by night.*

Alaska stretches high into the deep-frozen Arctic and includes empty wilderness, icy shores and some of the highest peaks in the Americas. The Hawaiian islands are really a chain of very high submarine volcanoes, with their tops emerging from the waves.

Cliff cascade
*The cliffs of California's Yosemite
Valley are braided with beautiful
waterfalls. This is the upper part
of the Yosemite Falls, the world's
second-highest, with a drop of
2,425 feet.*

Lava flow
*This slow-moving lava
from a Hawaiian volcano
is known as pahoehoe.*

Tornado twisters
*Raging whirlwinds called
tornadoes or twisters are
common in the Prairie
states. They can spin at
311 miles per hour.*

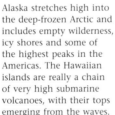

United States of America

DURING THE LAST 75 YEARS THE UNITED STATES HAS become the world's most powerful nation, and one of the richest.

It is a democratic republic which works on a federal system, with its states having powers to make their own laws. The head of state is a president, who is elected for a term of four years.

In addition to its 50 states, the USA also governs various island territories in the Pacific Ocean and the Caribbean Sea.

The United States is one of the world's great food producers, growing wheat, soya beans, maize, citrus fruits and vegetables. Coasts and rivers produce large catches of fish. Milwaukee is famous for its beers, Kentucky for its bourbon and California for its wines.

▲ Mount Rushmore
Completed in 1941, these giant heads show former presidents Washington, Jefferson, Roosevelt and Lincoln.

▲ All-American food
What's on the menu? As well as fast food such as hamburgers and hot dogs, the United States has given the world cola drinks, breakfast cereals and Florida orange juice.

The United States has great mineral wealth. It drills for oil and natural gas in Texas, the Gulf of Mexico and Alaska. It is the world's largest producer of coal. It has gold, uranium, copper and iron ore. Dammed rivers and lakes are used to produce hydroelectric power. Managed forests provide timber, with the far northwest a major center of logging.

◄ Early skyscrapers
The world's first skyscraper buildings were built in Chicago and New York City. Better known as the 'Flat Iron', New York's 20-storey Fuller Building was erected in 1901.

▲ Texas oil
Texas built its wealth on cattle, cotton and oil. Today, the United States ranks as the world's second largest oil producer.

▼ Biosphere 2
This experimental base was set up in the Arizona Desert. Inside, all of the Earth's habitats are recreated in miniature. It is a practice run for future space bases on other planets or on the Moon.

▲ The 'Big Apple'
New York City is home to over 7.5 million people. It is an exciting, high-speed town, a center for finance, business and the arts.

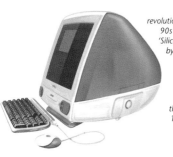

◄ Cyber success
The world computer revolution of the 1980s and 90s was spearheaded in 'Silicon Valley,' California by firms such as Apple and Microsoft.

► Disneyworld
This famous Florida theme park, opened in 1971, was the second one to be dreamt up by animated film pioneer Walt Disney.

American factories make a wide range of household goods, textiles and garments. California is the world center of computer technology and software, and also the center of the film and television industry. The United States is the leading manufacturer of airplanes and spacecraft. The city of Detroit makes cars.

◄ A Hollywood star
Stars are inset in the pavement in Hollywood, California, as a tribute to the big names of cinema. Walt Disney (1901–66) is honored as the creator of Mickey Mouse.

Services such as banking, finance and insurance are now more important to the American economy than manufacturing. New York City's Wall Street is the center of the American financial world. The United States, with neighboring Canada and Mexico, set up the North American Free Trade Agreement (NAFTA) in 1994.

Although the United States has such great economic power, it too has its problems. It faces increasing competition from other countries and has large debts.

▼ Shop till you drop!
American ways of buying and selling have spread around the world. Shopping malls are an American invention.

▲ Kennedy Space Center
A space shuttle blasts off on another mission from this launch site on Cape Canaveral, Florida.

▲ Harley Davidson
Electra Glide, 1988

23

United States of America

THREE-QUARTERS OF ALL AMERICANS
live in towns and cities.

Despite the wealth of the nation as a whole, many people in both city and country areas suffer from poverty.

The USA has no official religion, and yet religion plays a very important part in everyday life. Eighty-four percent of the population is Christian, with Protestants outnumbering Roman Catholics two to one. Judaism is the faith of two percent.

English is the official language, with Spanish widely spoken in some areas. The nation's first peoples (Native Americans, Inuit and Aleuts) now make up only one percent of the population. However there has been a strong revival of interest in their traditional cultures and in their rights as citizens.

▲ A free press
The United States has many famous city-based newspapers, including the Washington Post and the New York Times.

▲ Skating in Central Park
A haven for relaxation, Central Park lies at the heart of New York City's busy Manhattan district. It is a place to walk, jog, rollerblade or picnic.

▼ In Chinatown
Since the 1800s, the United States has had a large population of Chinese descent. In the Chinatown district of New York's Lower East Side, signs are in Chinese and shops sell Chinese food.

▲ Native American life
The first Americans still face many social and economic problems, but they have retained a fierce pride in their traditions and customs.

▲ Amish farmer

▼ Riding School, New Mexico
Horse-riding has been part of the American way of life since the days of the Wild West.

◀ **African Americans**
America's large black population is of African descent. Afro-Americans have played an important part in the advancement of civil rights and in American culture. They invented many popular musical forms, including jazz and the blues.

◀ **Fourth of July**
The United States marks its independence, won from Great Britain in 1776, each July 4th. This parade is taking place in the New England state of Maine.

The population as a whole comes from many different roots. The majority are Whites of European descent. These include English, Scots, Welsh, Irish, French, Italians, Germans, Dutch, Swedes and Poles. About nine percent are Hispanics, Spanish-speaking people originally from Mexico, Central America or the Caribbean. There are Jews, Chinese, Japanese, Koreans and Vietnamese. There are Polynesians from Hawaii and Samoa. About 12 percent of Americans are blacks of African and Caribbean descent, whose ancestors were enslaved by the European settlers during the first 300 years of settlement.

The minority peoples of the United States, from the Native Americans to the Afro-Americans, have all experienced racism and poverty. And yet the real wealth of the nation lies in the rich mixture of their cultures, in their music and dance, writing and art, customs and beliefs, food and festivals.

▲ **American fast foods**

▲ **Hawaiian dance**
The Hawaiian islands became a state of the Union in 1959. The islanders' dances and traditional costume belong to the Polynesian culture of the Pacific.

American writers, artists, musicians and film directors have had a great influence on the world during the last 100 years. Popular sports include baseball, basketball and football.

◀ **Hot gospel**
Christian Churches from the African tradition developed the choral sound known as gospel music, which also influenced popular music. This singer is also a New York City policewoman.

▼ **Home run**
Baseball is one of America's most popular sports. It has been played since the 1840s.

▲ ▶ **American football**
Fast and exciting, American football is popular both at college and at professional level. Superbowl contests have been known to attract world television audiences of over 138 million.

25

United States of America

THE NATIVE AMERICANS ARE DESCENDED from prehistoric peoples who crossed into North America from the Asian region of Siberia sometime after 30000BC. They developed many different cultures in different parts of the Americas.

In the 1500s colonists from Europe – English, Dutch, Spanish and French – began to explore and settle the east and south. At first they made alliances with the Native American peoples (whom they called 'Indians') but were soon entangled in bitter wars with them and with each other. Many Europeans purchased African slaves to work the land they had seized, planting tobacco and cotton.

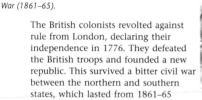

▲ Warring states
Flags of the Confederacy and the Union, the two conflicting sides in the American Civil War (1861–65).

The British colonists revolted against rule from London, declaring their independence in 1776. They defeated the British troops and founded a new republic. This survived a bitter civil war between the northern and southern states, which lasted from 1861–65 and brought an end to slavery.

▲ Fort Pitt
Nineteenth-century traders meet Native Americans at Fort Pitt. The Native Americans lost their lands and their way of life as European settlers moved West.

◄ Pilgrim Fathers
The most famous European settlers were a group of Puritans, religious refugees from England, who founded a colony at Plymouth Rock, Massachusetts, in 1620.

▼ A bitter conflict
Over 360,000 Union (northern) troops were killed during the Civil War, and 260,000 Confederate (southern) troops. Thousands of civilians also died.

▲ President Abe
Abraham Lincoln was 16th President of the United States. He was assassinated after the Confederate defeat, in 1865.

▼ Westward by wagon
In the 1840s thousands of pioneers headed west along routes such as the Oregon Trail, which stretched for 1,988 miles.

▲ The rush for gold
In 1848 gold was discovered on the American River, in California. Soon prospectors were arriving from all over the world in the hope of making their fortune.

◀ America mourns
John F Kennedy, a young and dynamic president, was assassinated in 1963. Here he is mourned by his wife Jackie and his brother, Robert.

The new country grew and grew. Pioneers pushed west into 'Indian Territory', seizing land and gunning down the Native American tribes. Vast areas of land were purchased from the French, Spanish and Russians (who governed Alaska until 1867). The east became industrialized, railways crossed the continent, gold was found in California. Thousands of poor people left Europe in search of fame and fortune in this new land.

The United States fought alongside the Allies in World War I, from 1917–18. After the boom years of the 1920s came an economic crash in 1929 and years of hardship. The United States was brought into World War II in 1941, when Japan bombed a naval base at Pearl Harbor, in the Hawaiian Islands.

▲ Martin Luther King
This great campaigner for civil rights won the Nobel Peace Prize in 1964, and was murdered in 1968.

After the end of the war in 1945, relations with one former ally, the communist Soviet Union, went from bad to worse. During this 'Cold War', the two rival powers remained on the brink of hostilities until the late 1980s.

▼ Political parties
The two most powerful political parties are the Democrats and Republicans. Here, Democrats hold their convention in Chicago.

AD	TIMELINE
1565	Spanish found St Augustine, Florida
1607	English found Jamestown, Virginia
1620	Pilgrim Fathers found Plymouth colony
1700s	Height of slave trade
1773	'Boston Tea Party'
1775	American Revolution
1776	Declaration of Independence
1783	Treaty of Paris: Britain loses colonies
1789	George Washington first president
1791	Bill of Rights
1803	Louisiana Purchase
1812	War with Britain (until 1814)
1819	Florida bought from Spain
1846	War with Mexico (until 1848): California and New Mexico gained
1861	Civil War (until 1865)
1865	President Lincoln assassinated
1867	Alaska bought from Russia
1876	Battle of the Little Big Horn
1890	Massacre at Wounded Knee
1898	Spanish-American War
1917	USA joins Allies against Central Powers in World War I (until 1918)
1929	Wall Street Crash: economic crisis
1941	Japan attacks Pearl Harbor: USA enters World War II on side of Allies (until 1945)
1950s	'Cold War' hostility towards Soviet Union (until 1990)
1961	USA in Vietnam War (until 1973)
1963	President John F Kennedy assassinated
1994	USA enters North American Free Trade Agreement (NAFTA)
1992	Bill Clinton elected President (re-elected 1996)

27

Mexico
and Central America

▶ **Hummingbird**
*Feathers shimmer as
this tiny bird sips nectar
from a tropical flower.*

Mexico's northern border runs along the banks of a river known in the United States as the Rio Grande and in Mexico as the Rio Bravo del Norte. It passes through hot, dusty desert.

◀ **Saguaro cactus**
*The saguaro of
Mexico's north-
western deserts is
the world's biggest
cactus, growing to
49 feet or more.*

A long, thin peninsula, Baja (Lower) California, extends southwards from Tijuana into the warm, blue Pacific Ocean. The Western and Eastern Sierra Madre ranges enclose a high central plateau, which includes deserts, lakes, swamps and smoking volcanoes. Violent earthquakes are common. Southern ranges include the Southern Sierra Madre and the Chiapas Highlands. In the far southeast, the Yucatán Peninsula forms a broad hook around the Bay of Campeche. In the south of the country, the vegetation includes lush, tropical forest.

The seven small countries of Central America lie to the south of the Isthmus of Tehuantepec. The landmass snakes from northwest to southeast, reaching its narrowest point at the Isthmus of Panama. Its backbone is a series of peaks, including many active volcanoes, and high plateaus or mesas. This highland chain is broken only by the expanse of Lake Nicaragua, which covers an area of 3,255 square miles. The Caribbean coastal strip is low-lying and flat, with swamps and lagoons. The Central American climate is tropical and often hot and humid.

▲ **Panama Canal**
*This vital shipping link was opened in
1914. It cuts through the Isthmus of
Panama to link the Atlantic and Pacific.*

◀ **Under
the volcano**
*Costa Rica is
a mountainous
country. The Arenal
Volcano, in the
Cordillera de
Guanacaste, last
erupted in 1968.*

FACTS

BELIZE
Republic of Belize
Area: *8,763 sq miles*
Population: *0.2 million*
Capital: *Belmopan*
Other cities: *Belize City, Dangriga*
Highest point: *Victoria Peak
(3,681 ft)*
Official language: *English*
Currency: *Belize dollar*

COSTA RICA
República de Costa Rica
Area: *197,30 sq miles*
Population: *3.4 million*
Capital: *San José*
Other cities: *Limón, Alajuela*
Highest point: *Chirripó Grande
(12,529 ft)*
Official language: *Spanish*
Currency: *Costa Rican colon*

EL SALVADOR
República de El Salvador
Area: *8,124 sq miles*
Population: *5.8 million*
Capital: *San Salvador*
Other cities: *Santa Ana, San Miguel*
Highest point: *Monte Cristo
(7,933 ft)*
Official language: *Spanish*
Currency: *Salvadorean colon*

GUATEMALA
República de Guatemala
Area: *42,042 sq miles*
Population: *10.9 million*
Capital: *Guatemala City*
Other cities: *Puerto Barrios,
Quezaltenango*
Highest point: *Tajumulco
(13,845 ft)*
Official language: *Spanish*
Currency: *quetzal*

▷ In Belize
The low-lying, swampy coast of Belize is fringed by coastal shallows and islands called cays. Hurricanes are common in August and September.

▲ Chichén itzá
This ruined city in Mexico's Yucatán peninsula was a center of the Mayan and Toltec civilizations between AD800 and 1180.

N
W **E**
S

MEXICO

UNITED STATES OF AMERICA

BELIZE

▲ After the hurricane
Much of Central America, including the Honduran capital, Tegucigalpa, was devastated by Hurricane Mitch in 1998.

GUATEMALA   HONDURAS

▲ Howler monkey
Some species of these large, noisy monkeys are threatened by the loss of tropical forests in Central American rainforests.

◁ Toucan
This bird's huge bill is used to eat tropical fruits.

MEXICO

PACIFIC
OCEAN

Bay of Campeche
Campeche
Veracruz
Villahermosa

Belize City
Belmopan
BELIZE
GUATEMALA   HONDURAS
Guatemala City   Tegucigalpa
San Salvador
EL SALVADOR   NICARAGUA
Managua   Nicaragua
Mosquitos
Gulf
San José   PANAMA
COSTA   Panama
RICA   City
Gulf of
Panama

NICARAGUA

EL SALVADOR

▲ Monarch butterfly

COSTA RICA

PANAMA

◁ Tropical forests
Large areas of the lush tropical forests which once covered Central America have been destroyed by loggers and farmers.

◁ Temple of the Warriors
This imposing ruin was built by the fierce Toltec warriors who conquered the Maya of Chichén Itzá in AD987.

Mexico and Central America

MEXICO IS NORMALLY CONSIDERED AS part of North America, although its southern regions have more in common with the Central American nations which lie to the south. It is a federal democratic republic and in 1994 signed up to the North American Free Trade Agreement (NAFTA) with Canada and the USA.

▲ Coffee beans
Coffee is a major export of Central American countries such as Nicaragua and Costa Rica.

Mexico has large oilfields in the Gulf of Mexico as well as silver, lead, gold and uranium. Ninety-five percent of its mineral resources are still to be mined. It manufactures fertilizers, petrochemicals, vehicles and machines. Mexican farmers grow cotton, coffee, tropical fruits and vegetables. There is a large fishing industry.

▲ Blue waters
Off Cajún, in northeast Yucatán, glass-bottomed boats allow tourists to see the wonders of a tropical coral reef.

Even so, Mexico faces many problems. It has the highest foreign debt of any developing country. Many of its people are very poor; over the years large numbers of them have crossed illegally into the United States in search of work. The population of Mexico City has soared above 20 million and it is probably the most polluted capital city in the world. In 1994 poor peasants in the southern state of Chiapas rose in rebellion against the central government.

▲ Sea harvest
A Mexican fisherman casts his net. Sardines are by far the largest catch in these waters, followed by anchovies, tuna and prawns.

▼ Down in Acapulco
Tourists flock to Acapulco in southwestern Mexico for the beaches and fishing. The city has one of the best natural harbors in the Pacific.

▲ Guacamole dip, tacos and chilli peppers

FACTS

HONDURAS
República de Honduras
Area: 43,277 sq miles
Population: 6.1 million
Capital: Tegucigalpa
Other cities: San Pedro Sula, Choluteca
Highest point: Cerro Las Minas (9,347 ft)
Official language: Spanish
Currency: lempira

MEXICO
Estados Unidos Mexicanos
Area: 756,061 sq miles
Population: 93.2 million
Capital: Mexico City
Other cities: Guadalajara, Monterrey, Puebla de Zaragoza
Highest point: Citlatépetl (18,701 ft)
Official language: Spanish
Currency: Mexican peso

NICARAGUA
República de Nicaragua
Area: 50,193 sq miles
Population: 4.5 million
Capital: Managua
Other cities: León, Granada
Highest point: Cordillera Isabella (7,999 ft)
Official language: Spanish
Currency: córdoba

PANAMA
República de Panamá
Area: 29,157 sq miles
Population: 2.7 million
Capital: Panama City
Other cities: San Miguelito, Colón, David
Highest point: Volcán Baru (11,401 ft)
Official language: Spanish
Currency: balboa

◄ Mexico City
The Mexican capital and its sprawling suburbs are home to nearly 25 million people. It is the most populous city in all the Americas and is a center of business, finance, industry and communications.

► Tropical produce
The tropical climate produces a variety of crops, with sugarcane grown in the humid lowlands and potatoes cultivated on cooler mountain slopes.

Mexico's problems are mirrored in the Central American republics of Guatemala, Belize, Honduras, El Salvador, Nicaragua, Costa Rica and Panama. Over the last 50 years, Central America suffered from extreme right-wing dictators and political parties, who have often tried to silence all opposition with death squads. These governments were sometimes backed by the United States, who wanted to prevent the region from becoming communist. The governments came under prolonged attack from left-wing revolutionaries. Central America also saw bitter disputes over territories and borders.

The root of all these conflicts has been grinding poverty. The warfare has now mostly ended, but the rebuilding process is very slow. Poverty and foreign debt remain the chief problem. The regional economy depends on coffee, bananas, cotton, sugarcane, maize, fish products and seafood. Exports include textiles and handicrafts.

▲ Banana trade
Bananas are packed for export before they ripen. The Central American countries compete fiercely with their Caribbean neighbors for their share of the world market.

▼ Market traditions
Bargain-hunters throng an outdoor flea market in Mexico City. The modern city is built on the site of the ancient Aztec capital, Tenochtitlán, which was famous for its vast, open-air markets.

▲ Woven by hand
The region is famous for its beautifully colored and patterned textiles. Traditionally, these are woven by hand, using simple backstrap looms.

► Mining for tin
Mexico has rich mineral reserves, including tin, silver, antimony, mercury and fluorite. Its most valuable reserves are of oil and natural gas.

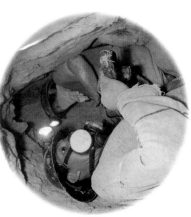

Mexico and Central America

FROM ABOUT 1200BC ONWARDS, MEXICO AND Central America saw the rise of many great civilizations founded by indigenous (native) peoples such as the Olmecs, Maya, Toltecs and Aztecs. Ruined cities, great pyramids and temples may still be seen. When the Spanish invaded the region in AD1519, they were awestruck by the wonders of the Aztec capital, Tenochtitlán (today's Mexico City).

The indigenous peoples, whom the Spanish called 'Indians', were skilled astronomers, mathematicians, writers, musicians and craftspeople. However they had no firearms and so were soon defeated. The region became part of Spain's overseas empire for the next three hundred years or so.

After independence in 1823, power remained in the hands of a few wealthy landowners. Mexico lost large areas of territory to the United States in the 1840s. From 1910 until 1917 the country was torn apart by revolution and civil war.

▲ **An Olmec head**
This colossal stone head was carved about three thousand years ago by the Olmec people of ancient Mexico.

▲ **An Aztec headdress**
The Aztecs were fine craftworkers, producing beautiful feather cloaks and headdresses, intricate jewellery and finely-patterned textiles.

▼ **Colonial architecture**
Spanish-built churches may still be seen in Taxco de Alarcón, Mexico. The region was already a center of mining before the Spanish came here in 1528.

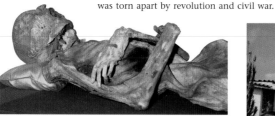

▲ **Mexican mummies**
Peoples of ancient Mexico, such as the Aztecs and Mixtecs, bundled up mummies of the dead. These might be burned or buried.

◀ **Mitla ruins**
Mitla, in southern Mexico, was an ancient holy site. It was occupied by the Mixtecs about a thousand years ago. Its ruins still bear traces of the original paint, made from berries.

▼ **The Maya**
The classic period of Mayan civilization lasted from about AD250 to 900. It was marked by the building of cities with great stone temples and pyramids. The homeland of the Maya stretched from Mexico's Yucatán peninsula southwards into Guatemala and Belize. Their descendants still live in these regions today.

◀ **Textile weaving**
Skeins of brilliant colored wools are piled up high ready for sale in this Guatemalan market place.

▼ **Fiesta!**
Festivals are an important part of both Spanish and local traditions in Mexico.

◀ **Violinist**
Mariachi music originated in Jalisco, Mexico. Sentimental songs are played on violins, guitars and trumpets.

After the Central American nations gained independence, they at first tried to unite in a federation. However they went their separate ways in 1838. Here too, the people remained desperately poor while a few landowners grew very rich. Belize was a British colony called British Honduras from 1862 until 1981.

Despite a troubled history, the peoples of the region enjoy a rich culture. Some are of European descent, but these are outnumbered by mestizos, people of mixed native and Spanish descent. Indigenous peoples still living in the region include large groups of Maya, as well as Otomi, Tarascan, Zapotec, Mixtec, Tarahumara, Nahua, Miskito, Guaymi and Cuna. The Garifuna, who live in Belize, Honduras and Nicaragua, are descended from Africans and from an indigenous people called the Caribs. The whole region is Spanish-speaking. Indigenous languages are also spoken and English is heard in Belize and on Nicaragua's east coast.

Mexico and Central America are strongly Roman Catholic, although indigenous traditions have influenced many colorful religious festivals and processions.

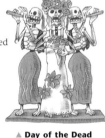

▲ **Day of the Dead**
Mexicans commemorate their dead each year on November 1st. Altars are laden with food offerings, papier-mâché skeletons, photographs and flowers.

▼ **Mixed traditions**
Ancient Mayan rituals have influenced the Christian worship of the Quiché Maya, of Guatemala.

TIMELINE

BC	
c.2600	Origins of Maya civilization in Yucatán
c.1000	Origins of Zapotec civilization
AD	
300s	Mayan empire (until 900s)
c.1325	Aztecs build great city of Tenochtitlán
1400s	Height of Aztec empire
1519	Spain invades Aztec empire (conquers Aztecs by 1521 and goes on to colonize all Central America)
1600s	Pirate attacks on Atlantic coast
1810	Revolt against Spanish rule in Mexico
1821	Collapse of Spanish rule in Central America
1823	United provinces of Central America (by 1838): Honduras, Costa Rica, El Salvador, Guatemala, Nicaragua
1846	Mexican War with USA (until 1848): loss of California and New Mexico
1862	British Honduras (Belize) a British colony
1911	Mexican Revolution: political reform
1914	Panama Canal opens
1970s	Political violence in Guatemala
1978	Nicaraguan Revolution
1981	Belize independent
1985	Earthquake, Mexico City
1994	Uprising in Chiapas, Mexico
	Mexico enters North American Free Trade Agreement (NAFTA)
1998	Hurricane Mitch

The Caribbean

▼ **Tropical beach, St Lucia**
St Lucia is a volcanic island lying in the Windward Islands. Its white-sand beaches and spectacular scenery attract many tourists.

Many beautiful islands lie between the Straits of Florida and the Venezuelan coast of South America. They are bordered in the west by the Gulf of Mexico and in the east by the open Atlantic. Many of the islands are formed from coral or from volcanic rock. Some have active volcanoes. Offshore reefs form spectacular underwater worlds of corals, seaweeds and brilliantly-colored fish.

The climate is generally tropical and warm, with the humidity relieved by ocean breezes on the smaller islands. Fierce storms called hurricanes bring high winds and rains in late summer and autumn.

The Bahamas and the Turks and Caicos islands form the northern, outer ring of islands. The Greater Antilles chain includes Cuba, the largest island of the region. It has fertile plains, rolling hills, forests and mountains. Its neighbors are the Cayman Islands, Jamaica, Hispaniola (divided between Haiti and the Dominican Republic) and Puerto Rico.

The islands of the Lesser Antilles are smaller, scattered around a great arc between the Virgin Islands and Aruba. The northern ones are known as the Leeward Islands and the southern ones as the Windward Islands. The area enclosed by the Antilles is called the Caribbean Sea.

► **Scarlet ibis**

▲ **Donkey traffic**
Donkeys are a traditional way of getting around in the mountainous countryside of the Dominican Republic.

FACTS

ANTIGUA AND BARBUDA
Area: 171 sq miles
Population: 64,000
Capital: St Johns
Highest point: Boggy Peak (1,319 ft)
Official language: English
Currency: East Caribbean dollar

BAHAMAS
Commonwealth of the Bahamas
Area: 5,358 sq miles
Population: 0.27 million
Capital: Nassau
Highest point: Cat Island (207 ft)
Official language: English
Currency: Bahamian dollar

BARBADOS
Area: 166 sq miles
Population: 0.26 million
Capital: Bridgetown
Highest point: Mt Hillaby (1,115 ft)
Official language: English
Currency: Barbados dollar

CUBA
República de Cuba
Area: 42,803 sq miles
Population: 11.0 million
Capital: Havana
Other cities: Santiago de Cuba, Camagüey
Highest point: Turquino (6,578 ft)
Official language: Spanish
Currency: Cuban peso

▼ Stormy weather
Satellites in space track the progress of a hurricane. These devastating, whirling storms sweep across the Caribbean between August and October each year.

▲ Palm trees
Everyone's image of the Caribbean is of beautiful palm trees swaying in the breeze. Here, on the sunny island of Jamaica, coconuts are growing in trees that can be as tall as 78.7 feet.

CUBA

BAHAMAS

PUERTO RICO

ANTIGUA AND BARBUDA

ST KITTS AND NEVIS

DOMINICA

ST LUCIA

JAMAICA

HAITI

DOMINICAN REPUBLIC

TRINIDAD AND TOBAGO

GRENADA

ST VINCENT AND THE GRENADINES

BARBADOS

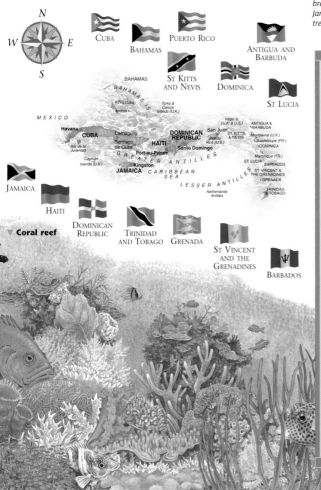

▼ Coral reef

FACTS

DOMINICA
Commonwealth of Dominica
Area: 290 sq miles
Population: 0.07 million
Capital: Roseau
Highest point: Morne Diablotin (4,747 ft)
Official language: English
Currency: East Caribbean dollar

DOMINICAN REPUBLIC
República Dominicana
Area: 18,816 sq miles
Population: 8.0 million
Capital: Santo Domingo
Other cities: Santiago de los Caballeros, La Romana
Highest point: Pico Duarte (10,417 ft)
Official language: Spanish
Currency: Dominican Republic peso

GRENADA
Area: 133 sq miles
Population: 0.1 million
Capital: St George's
Highest point: Mt St Catherine (2,756 ft)
Official language: English
Currency: East Caribbean dollar

HAITI
République d'Haïti
Area: 10,714 sq miles
Population: 7.3 million
Capital: Port-au-Prince
Other cities: Jacmel, Les Cayes
Highest point: La Selle (8,783 ft)
Official languages: French, Creole
Currency: gourde

The Caribbean

THERE ARE 13 INDEPENDENT NATIONS IN
the Caribbean region. Some are democratic
republics, some still have European
monarchs as their heads of state.
Economic links are strengthened by the
Caribbean Community and Common
Market (Caricom, founded in 1973).
Most of the Caribbean's 11 other territories
remain dependencies of other countries by
choice, because it brings them wealth or security.
Some are governed as if they were
part of mainland France.

▲ **World-class cigars**
*Cuba has long been famous for
the finest quality cigars and for
rum, made from sugarcane.*

▲ **Che Guevara**
*Argentinian-born
Ernesto 'Che' Guevara
played an important
part in the Cuban
revolution (1956–9).
He was killed in Bolivia
in 1967.*

Cuba, the largest Caribbean island, has had a
communist government since 1959. This has been
bitterly opposed by the United States. Until 1991,
Cuba had vital trading links with the communist
countries of Central and Eastern Europe. Since
then, Cuba has had to struggle against a strict
United States ban on trade.

Political violence and corruption
have a long history on some islands,
such as Haiti. On other islands the
problem has been one of alliances.
For example, Anguilla refused to join
the federation of St Kitts–Nevis when
it became independent, and Aruba
pulled out of the Netherlands
Antilles. Other islands have been
hard hit by natural disasters, such
as hurricane damage or volcanic
eruptions.

▲ **Fidel Castro**
*The leader of Cuba's revolution
was Fidel Castro. He overthrew
the corrupt regime of Fulgencio
Batista in 1959 and was still
Cuban president 40 years later.*

▲ **Radio telescope**
*The world's biggest
single-unit radio
telescope is located
near Arecibo, on the
island of Puerto Rico.*

◄ **Boat building**
*A wooden hull is
constructed in
Barbados. Boats are
still built by traditional
methods on many
Caribbean islands.*

FACTS

JAMAICA
Area: 4,243 sq miles
Population: 2.5 million
Capital: Kingston
*Other cities: Spanish Town,
Montego Bay*
*Highest point: Blue Mountain Peak
(7,401 ft)*
Official language: English
Currency: Jamaican dollar

ST KITTS – NEVIS
Federation of St Christopher and Nevis
Area: 101 sq miles
Population: 0.04 million
Capital: Basseterre
Highest point: Liamuiga (3,793 ft)
Official language: English
Currency: East Caribbean dollar

ST LUCIA
Area: 240 sq miles
Population: 0.16 million
Capital: Castries
Highest point: Mt Gimie (3,146 ft)
Official language: English
Currency: East Caribbean dollar

ST VINCENT AND THE GRENADINES
Area: 150 sq miles
Population: 0.11 million
Capital: Kingstown
*Highest point: La Soufrière
(4,173 ft)*
Official language: English
Currency: East Caribbean dollar

TRINIDAD AND TOBAGO
Republic of Trinidad and Tobago
Area: 1,981 sq miles
Population: 1.3 million
Capital: Port-of-Spain
Other cities: San Fernando, Arima
Highest point: Aripo (3,084 ft)
Official language: English
*Currency: Trinidad and
Tobago dollar*

◀ **Market day**
What's on sale in a Caribbean market? Lush tropical fruits, coconuts, saltfish, seafood and vegetables. Snacks on offer are sure to include rotis – pancakes wrapped around curried chicken and vegetables.

▼ **Changing times**
St Lucia's Rodney Bay was once a swampy coastline with a couple of fishing villages. In the 1940s, it was transformed into a US naval airbase. Today, it is a tourist center, with a yachting marina and many hotels.

Many of the Caribbean islanders are poor. Cash crops, produced for export, include spices, tropical fruits such as bananas, mangoes and limes, sugarcane and cotton. Cuba is famous for its rum and tobacco. Many islanders fish and grow their own food. Popular local dishes are made from saltfish, pigeon peas, coconut, chilli peppers, and cornmeal.

Manufacturing is limited, but Trinidad produces oil and natural gas. The region's blue seas and beaches of white sand fringed with palms have made tourism a major industry in many islands. Other islands, such as the Caymans, have passed tax laws which allow international finance companies and banks to set up their headquarters there. The wealth made from tourism and offshore banking often fails to benefit the local people.

▲ **Sailfish**
With a pointed bill and a sail-like fin, this powerful fish can reach speeds of up to 49.7 miles per hour.

▼ **Caribbean village**
Most Caribbeans live in simple, one-storey homes. White walls reflect the sun and keep the interiors cool despite the fierce heat outside. Up to four generations of the same family may live together in one or these small houses.

FACTS

Caribbean dependencies

ANGUILLA
British Overseas Territory
Area: *35 sq miles*
Population: *9,000*
Capital: *The Valley*
Official language: *English*
Currency: *East Caribbean dollar*

ARUBA
Self-governing island of the Netherlands
Area: *75 sq miles*
Population: *0.08 million*
Capital: *Oranjestad*
Official language: *Dutch*
Currency: *Aruban guilder*

CAYMAN ISLANDS
British Overseas Territory
Area: *102 sq miles*
Population: *0.03 million*
Capital: *George Town*
Official language: *English*
Currency: *Cayman Islands dollar*

GUADELOUPE
Overseas region of France
Area: *658 sq miles*
Population: *0.4 million*
Capital: *Basse-Terre*
Official language: *French*
Currency: *French franc*

MARTINIQUE
Overseas region of France
Area: *425 sq miles*
Population: *0.4 million*
Capital: *Fort-de-France*
Official language: *French*
Currency: *French franc*

The Caribbean

IN PREHISTORIC TIMES THE CARIBBEAN ISLANDS WERE settled by indigenous peoples from the American mainland. When Columbus discovered the islands in 1492, these formed two main groups – Arawak-speaking peoples and Caribs. The Arawaks were savagely treated by the invaders. They were enslaved, murdered or infected with diseases. The Caribs, who had a fearsome reputation amongst the Europeans, resisted longer. In the end, however, few communities survived.

▶ **Arawak art**
The Arawak-speaking peoples of the Caribbean carved figures from stone.

The Spanish took over many islands. As their fleets shipped back plundered treasures from the mainland (the 'Spanish Main'), they were preyed on by British, French and Dutch pirates. Soon these countries too seized islands and planted them with tobacco or sugarcane. They imported slaves from Africa to work the land. Cruelly treated, some slaves escaped and there were violent revolts in Jamaica and Haiti in the 1700s. In the 1800s, Haiti became the first independent Afro-Caribbean republic.

▲ **The Santa Maria**
Christopher Columbus' ship reached San Salvador, in the Bahamas, in 1492 – a turning point in American history.

▼ **The slave trade**
Slavery was the curse of the Caribbean from the 1500s until its abolition three centuries later. Slaves were sold like cattle, families were separated and punishments were harsh, often fatal.

▲ **Sugar plantations**
Sugarcane dominated the Caribbean economy from the 1600s until recent times. Sugar was shipped to Europe and North America. The backbreaking labor on the European-owned plantations was carried out by slaves imported from West Africa.

◀ **Haitian voodoo**
Drums and dancing send people into a trance at Cap Haitien. Voodoo, known as Vodun in the Creole dialect of Haiti, is based on an African belief in spirits called loas. It inspired the slave revolts on Haiti and is still popular today.

FACTS

MONTSERRAT
British Overseas Territory
Area: 39.4 sq miles
Population: 0.01 million (6,000 since volcanic eruptions of 1995–7)
Capital: Plymouth (evacuated)
Official language: English
Currency: East Caribbean dollar

NETHERLANDS ANTILLES
Self-governing islands of the Netherlands
Area: 309 sq miles
Population: 0.2 million
Capital: Willemstad
Official language: Dutch
Currency: Netherlands Antilles guilder

PUERTO RICO
Commonwealth territory of the USA
Area: 3,427 sq miles
Population: 3.8 million
Capital: San Juan
Official languages: English, Spanish
Currency: US dollar

TURKS AND CAICOS ISLANDS
British Overseas Territory
Area: 166 sq miles
Population: 0.01 million
Capital: Cockburn Town
Official language: English
Currency: US dollar

VIRGIN ISLANDS (BRITISH)
British Overseas Territory
Area: 58 sq miles
Population: 0.02 million
Capital: Road Town
Official language: English
Currency: US dollar

VIRGIN ISLANDS (USA)
Unincorporated Territory of the USA
Area: 134 sq miles
Population: 0.1 million
Capital: Charlotte Amalie
Official language: English
Currency: US dollar

▼ Steel band
Steel drums called pans provide the typical sound of Trinidad.

▶ Carnival
Carnival in Trinidad is a time of glitzy costumes, dancing, steel-band music and verses called calypsos.

▲ Pirate women
Two notorious women pirates, Anne Bonny and Mary Read, went on trial in Jamaica in 1720. Caribbean coasts had long been terrorized by pirates and buccaneers.

After the abolition of slavery (mostly in the 1830s) many European settlers left the region they called the West Indies. At the same time laborers from India and Southeast Asia were hired to work on some islands, such as Trinidad. Most Caribbean islands remained colonies until the 1960s.

Today's Caribbeans are descended from many roots – Native American, African, Spanish, English, Irish, French, Dutch and Asian. Much the largest ethnic groups are of Afro-Caribbean or Hispanic descent. Spanish, English and French are widely spoken, often in strong Creole dialects influenced by African languages. The region is strongly Christian, with some followers of African spirit religions, such as the Voodoo worship on Haiti. The Rastafarians of Jamaica are also inspired by African spirituality.

The Caribbean's mixed roots have inspired a range of popular music and dance styles that have become popular all over the world, from salsa to reggae. Music comes to the fore in the region's famous carnivals. Popular sports include cricket, soccer and baseball.

▲ Cricket
West Indian cricket teams have been world-beaters since the 1960s.

◀ Back to Africa
Rastafarians look back to their African roots and honor Haile Selassie (1891–1975), former emperor of Ethiopia.

AD	TIMELINE
c.200	Native American settlement: Ciboney people expelled from Cuba by the Taíno
c.1000	Arawak and Carib migrations and wars
1492	Christopher Columbus lands in the Bahamas
1496	First Spanish settlement, Santo Domingo (Hispaniola)
1511	Spanish settle Cuba
1523	Slave trade with Africa
1655	British capture Jamaica
1660s	Piracy widespread (until 1720s)
1697	French gain control of Haiti (Hispaniola)
1804	Haiti independent republic under black rule
1838	Abolition of slave trade in some parts of the region
1868	Independence movement defeated in Cuba (by 1878)
1895	Uprising in Cuba (until 1898)
1898	Puerto Rico ceded to USA
1952	Fulgencio Batista seizes power in Cuba
1959	Fidel Castro overthrows Batista in Cuba
1961	Barbados independent
1962	Cuban Missile Crisis: clash with USA over siting of Soviet missile base Jamaica, Trinidad independent
1973	Bahamas independent
1983	USA invades Grenada
1995	Series of volcanic eruptions begins on Montserrat

Americas

Northern Andean countries

The Andes mountains run down the whole length of South America, from Colombia to Tierra del Fuego, a distance of over 3,977 miles. The mountains are very high, very beautiful and very valuable, for they contain precious silver, tin and other minerals.

▲ **Condor**

The range includes massive snow-capped volcanoes, gleaming glaciers and wide, cool plateaus. Titicaca, the world's highest navigable lake, occupies 3,200 square miles of the plateau on the border between Peru and Bolivia.

To the north, the Andes drop to low-lying plains around the humid Caribbean coast. To the west, they are bordered by a coastal strip along the Pacific Ocean. In parts this is humid and fertile, but in Peru much of it is dusty desert. That is because cold ocean currents make it more difficult for the air to fill with moisture and form rain. Far to the west, Ecuador also takes in a Pacific island chain, the Galápagos.

▲ **Bird and snake**
Beautiful stone carvings were produced at San Augustín, Colombia, about 2,000 years ago.

To the east, the peaks and sunlit plateaus of the Andes descend through misty foothills and sheer-sided valleys into the vast rainforests of central South America. Streams rising on the eastern slopes drain into the great Orinoco and Amazon river systems.

▼ **Buttress roots**

▲ **One more river**
The Urubamba rises in the Andes and flows through deep gorges. It eventually joins up with the Apurímac to form the Ucayali, which in turn drains into the mighty Amazon.

FACTS

BOLIVIA
República de Bolivia
Area: 424,162 sq miles
Population: 7.6 million
Capitals: La Paz, Sucre
Other cities: Santa Cruz, Cochabamba
Highest point: Nevado Sajama (21,463 ft)
Official language: Spanish
Currency: peso boliviano

COLOMBIA
República de Colombia
Area: 439,735 sq miles
Population: 37.4 million
Capital: Bogotá
Other cities: Medellín, Cali, Barranquilla
Highest point: Cristobal Colón (18,947 ft)
Official language: Spanish
Currency: Colombian peso

ECUADOR
República del Ecuador
Area: 178,175 sq miles (including Galápagos Islands)
Population: 11.7 million
Capital: Quito
Other cities: Guayaquil, Cuenca
Highest point: Chimborazo (20,561 ft)
Official language: Spanish
Currency: sucre

PERU
República de Peru
Area: 496,222 sq miles
Population: 24.3 million
Capital: Lima
Other cities: Callao, Arequipa, Chiclayo
Highest point: Nevado Huascarán (22,204 ft)
Official languages: Spanish, Quechua, Aymará
Currency: nuevo sol

▲ **Baños, Ecuador**
This small town lies in the eastern Andes, on the route to El Oriente, Ecuador's province in the Amazon River basin.

▶ **Andes watershed**
South America is divided into two by the Andes range. Some rainfall drains into the Pacific Ocean, but the rest flows eastwards into the distant Atlantic.

COLOMBIA

ECUADOR

Point. Gallinas
Barranquilla
Cartagena
Cristobal Colón 5,775 m
PANAMA
Cauca
Magdalena
VENEZUELA
Cape Corrientes
Medellín
Pereira Manizales
Ibagué Bogotá
Meta
Buenaventura **COLOMBIA**
Cali Neiva
Nevado del Huila 5,750 m
Pasto
Guaviare
Point Galera
Quito
ECUADOR
Caquetá
Guayaquil Chimborazo 6,267 m
Gulf of Guayaquil
Putumayo
Amazon
Iquitos
Point Aguja
Piura Marañón
Chiclayo
BRAZIL
Trujillo
Chimbote Nevado Huascarán 6,768 m
Callao
Lima Huancayo
PERU
Cuzco
Paracas Pen.
Nazca Volcán El Misti 5,842 m
Nevado Ancohuma
Arequipa Lake Titicaca **La Paz**
BOLIVIA
Mamoré
Guaporé
Cochabamba
PACIFIC OCEAN
Oruro Santa Cruz
Lake Poopó Sucre
ALTIPLANO
Potosí Pilcomayo
CHILE
PARAGUAY

N
W E
S

BOLIVIA

PERU

◀ **River of ice**
In Peru, the Andes divide into three main sections. The highest peaks rise in the Cordillera Blanca. Here, snow-capped peaks tower above glaciers such as Pastoruri, at 17,388 feet above sea level.

▲ **Eastern Bolivia**
This hamlet lies in the Las Yungas region of eastern Bolivia, where the Altiplano (high plateau) drops to the humid, forested lowlands of the Amazon basin.

▼ **Lake Titicaca**
This is the largest lake in South America. It is really made up of two smaller lakes, Chucuito and Uinamarca, which are linked by a narrow strait.

▶ **Llama**
For thousands of years the llama has provided wool and meat, as well as being used to carry loads over high Andean passes.

◀ **High altitude**
The Chacaltuya ski lodge near La Paz, Bolivia, is the world's highest. It overlooks the tablelands of the Altiplano. 41

Northern Andean countries

THE FOUR COUNTRIES OF THE NORTHERN ANDES
are all republics. The army has often
seized power in this region, or
controlled governments behind the
scenes. There have been long
years of guerrilla warfare, fuelled
by widespread poverty and social
injustice. There have been
murderous activities by the criminal
gangs who export cocaine. This illegal
drug is made from the coca plant,
which has been grown by poor
peasants in the region for
thousands of years.

▲ **Cocaine patrol**
A plane hunts for secret coca
plantations. This plant, used as
a drug for thousands of years,
is processed to make cocaine.

▲ **Mule train**
Surefooted but stubborn,
mules have been used to
transport goods in the
Andes since the 1500s.

The northern Andes region has great mineral
wealth in the form of oil, copper, emeralds,
silver, tin, zinc, lead, silver and gold. However
many people remain very poor, in both city
and country areas. In the hot, lowlands, farmers
grow cotton, sugarcane and
bananas. Colombian coffee beans,
grown on tropical slopes, are
among the best in the world.
On the the cool plateaus, potatoes,
maize, wheat and a grain called
quinoa are grown.

The forests produce valuable
timber. Sardines, anchovies
and tuna are caught by the large
Pacific fishing fleets. Shrimps are
farmed along the coast. Fish are
also processed to make fertilizers.

▲ **Farming the slopes**
Farmers were already terracing
the steep Andean slopes in
ancient times, in order to
conserve soil. The Incas were
masters of irrigation techniques.

▲ **Silver mountain**
When the Spanish
conquered Bolivia, Cerro
Rico, in Potosi, became the
world's biggest silver mine.
The riches were shipped
back to Europe.

▼ **Andean station**
Alausí, a center of population
in Ecuador's Chimborazo
province, is built on the
Guayaquil–Quito railway.
The world's highest railways
are in the Andes, in Peru.

◄ **Upriver**
Motorized canoes travel
along the Río Aguarico,
which and flows through
eastern Ecuador.

▲ **The fur trade**
In Colombia, illegal
hunting claims the lives of
many rare wildlife species,
such as the ocelot.

Lima stadium
Peru's National Stadium is sited in Lima, the capital. Lima is home to nearly six million people.

The region is strongly Roman Catholic and there are many religious festivals and pilgrimages. Spanish is spoken in all four countries. There are many people of mestizo (mixed European and Indian) as well as a number of European, African or Asian descent. Indigenous (native) peoples make up just one percent of the population in Colombia, but 25 percent in Ecuador, 45 percent in Peru, and 55 percent in Bolivia.

The two largest indigenous groups are the Aymara and Quechua. Most of these 'Indians' are poor peasants and are largely ignored by those who hold power in the cities. In the mountains, life carries on as it has for centuries, with the local people weaving, going to market and herding llamas. The haunting folk music of the Andes is played on guitars, panpipes, flutes and drums.

▲ Local transport
A motorized rickshaw provides transport in Chiclayo, the chief town of Peru's Lambayeque region. It lies on the Pan-American highway, the road network which links North to South America.

▼ Columbian capital
Mountains rise behind Bogotá's modern high-rise skyline. Colombia's chief city is home to some five million people.

◄ Straw hats
Ecuador manufactures panama hats. These are woven from the leaves of a palm-like shrub called jipyapa.

► Bamboo pipes
Known as antaras or zampoñas, panpipes have been played since the days of the Incas.

► Fishing boats
The Aymara and Uru peoples of Lake Titicaca make fishing boats called balsas from reeds. Fish caught in this deep lake include catfish, trout and killifish.

◄ Gathering reeds
Tall, tough reeds called totora grow on the shores and islands of Lake Titicaca and on floating platforms of vegetation. They are harvested and made into houses as well as fishing boats.

43

Northern Andean countries

DESPITE ITS JAGGED MOUNTAIN PEAKS, VOLCANOES and deserts, the northern Andes region was settled by the waves of tribes who peopled the Americas in prehistoric times. It became the site of many very advanced ancient civilizations.

From about 1200BC until 200BC the Chavín civilization produced stone carvings, pottery and painted textiles. Strange lines scratched deep into the desert near Nazca in southern Peru may have been designed to honor the gods. Further north, the Moche valley was the center of a civilization which built pyramids in honor of the Sun, and engineered an irrigation system for crops in dry regions.

▲ **Tiahuanaco**
The city of Tiahuanaco, in the Bolivian Andes, flourished from about AD100 until 1250.

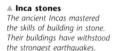

▲ **Inca stones**
The ancient Incas mastered the skills of building in stone. Their buildings have withstood the strongest earthquakes.

Over 1,000 years ago, the Chimú people of northern Peru were masters of working gold and they also produced pottery on a large scale. The most amazing civilization of all was that of the Incas, who defeated the Chimú in AD1476. The Inca empire, with its capital at Cuzco in Peru, stretched from Ecuador to Chile and took in about 12 million people. The Incas were builders of cities and towns, who studied the stars and built great temples.

▲ **Peruvian funeral mask**

▶ **Machu Picchu**
This lost city of the Incas, high above the gorges of the Urubamba, was rediscovered in 1911.

▶ **Pilgrimage**
The Spanish conquerors brought Roman Catholicism to the Andes. This is the Sanctuary of Nuestra Señora de Acua Santa, in Ecuador.

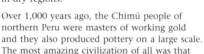

▲ **Temple of the Sun**
This pyramid dominated the Moche capital. 131 feet high, it is believed to contain about 140 million mud bricks.

▶ **Conquest**
The Spanish reached Peru in 1532. They captured the emperor, Atahualpa, by treachery and soon conquered all the Inca lands, although resistance continued for 40 years.

◀ **Quito, Ecuador**
The capital of Ecuador has old colonial buildings alongside modern offices and factories. The city is built at 9,350 feet above sea level, beneath the Pichincha volcano.

▲ **La Paz, Bolivia**
A street vendor sells vegetables in La Paz, one of Bolivia's twin capitals. La Paz is the world's highest capital, at 11,913 feet.

Spain invaded Colombia in 1499. By 1532 a small force of Spanish soldiers, called conquistadors, had used treachery to overthrow the powerful Inca empire to the south. They were greedy for gold and silver, and the northern Andes offered wealth beyond their dreams.

▲ **Lure of gold**
The Spanish were first attracted to South America by rumors of fabulous gold.

Spain's rule over the region lasted nearly 300 years. They built churches and cities, mined for silver and used the indigenous people to labor on the land. In the 1820s a revolutionary called Simón Bolívar (1783–1830) led the struggle against continuing rule by Spain. His name was taken up by one of the territories he freed, Bolivia.

The newly-independent countries were soon attacking each other. Wealth remained within a few families of the ruling class, while most people remained wretchedly poor into modern times.

▶ **Mountain dress**
Many Bolivians still wear traditional dress, including blankets, shawls and these distinctive bowler hats.

◀ **Inca trail**
The Inca empire was linked by a vast network of roads, bridges and mountain trails. Goods were carried by llama. Relays of runners carried messages by hand.

TIMELINE

BC	
8500	Possible origins of farming in Peru
3000	Pottery made in Colombia and Ecuador
1500	Metalworking in Peru
900	Chavín civilization in Andes
200	Nazca civilization, Peru
AD	
1	Moche civilization, Peru
600	Tiahuanaco civilization, Bolivia
1200	Beginnings of Inca empire
1250	Chimu civilization, Peru
1400s	Inca empire at greatest extent
1531	Spanish land in Ecuador
1533	Incas defeated by Spanish
1538	Colombia conquered by Spanish
1545	Silver mining in Bolivia
1780	Indigenous uprising in Peru
1819	Colombia independent from Spain
1822	Ecuador joins Colombia
1824	Peru independent from Spain
1825	Bolivia independent from Spain
1830	Full independence for Colombia Ecuador independent
1884	Bolivia loses Atacama to Chile
1932	Chaco War (until 1935): Bolivia defeated by Paraguay
1941	Peru invades Ecuador
1948	OAS (Organization of American States) is signed at Bogotá, Colombia
1952	Bolivian National Revolution
1989	Drug gang violence in Colombia

Brazil
and its neighbors

◀ Poison-
arrow frog

Venezuela ('Little Venice') was given its name because the vast, shallow inlet of Lake Maracaibo reminded early European explorers of the lagoons around Venice, in Italy.

Venezuela is dominated by the river Orinoco, which forces its way between a northern spur of the Andes Mountains and the Guiana Highlands. It flows through the grassy plains of the Llanos to form a wide, swampy delta on the Caribbean coast. In the central southeast, the Angel Falls form the world's highest waterfall, with a total drop of 3,212 feet.

▲ **Anteater**
There are three South American anteater species. All have long, sticky tongues, for eating ants and termites.

The low-lying Caribbean coast, with a hot and sticky climate, continues eastwards through Guyana, Surinam and French Guiana. In the south of these countries the land rises to the forested slopes of the Guiana Highlands.

▲ **Big river**
The Amazon is the world's second-longest river, after the Nile, with a total length of over 3,977 miles.

Across the Brazilian border, these descend to the great basin of the Amazon River. This mighty river is fed by thousands of waterways which seep through the tropical growth of the world's largest rainforest, covering an area of over 825 million acres. Broad and muddy, the Amazon flows eastwards to the Atlantic Ocean. Southern Brazil rises to the Brazilian Highlands and the tropical plateau of the Matto Grosso. This is drained in the south by the river Paraná.

FACTS

BRAZIL
República Federativa do Brasil
Area: 3,300,152 sq miles
Population: 161.2 million
Capital: Brasília
Other cities: São Paulo, Rio de Janeiro, Salvador, Belo Horizonte, Pôrto Alegre
Highest point: Neblina (9,888 ft)
Official language: Portuguese
Currency: cruzeiro real

GUYANA
Co-operative Republic of Guyana
Area: 83,000 sq miles
Population: 0.8 million
Capital: Georgetown
Other cities: New Amsterdam, Linden
Highest point: Roraima (9,094 ft)
Official language: English
Currency: Guyana dollar

SURINAM
Republic of Suriname
Area: 63,037 sq miles
Population: 0.4 million
Capital: Paramaribo
Other cities: Groningen, Nieuw Amsterdam
Highest point: Juliana Top (4,035 ft)
Official language: Dutch
Currency: Surinam guilder

◀ **Palms in the Pantanal**
In southwestern Brazil, the Pantanal wetlands are created by the seasonal flooding of the Paraguay River. The waters cover about 38,996 square kilometres of the Matto Grosso.

◀ Iguaçu Falls
The Iguaçu River plunges over hundreds of waterfalls and rocks before it joins the Paraná on the Brazil-Argentina border.

▲ Devil's Island
Just off the coast of French Guiana, this popular tourist resort was once a French prison colony.

VENEZUELA

GUYANA

SURINAM

FRENCH GUIANA

BRAZIL

Netherlands Antilles
Gulf of Venezuela
Caracas
Port of Spain **TRINIDAD & TOBAGO** GUYANA
Maracaibo
Barcelona
Lake Maracaibo ANDES MTS.
LLANOS
Orinoco
Orinoco Delta
Pico Bolívar 5,002 m
VENEZUELA
Angel Falls
Georgetown
Paramaribo
COLOMBIA
GUIANA
GUYANA
Cayenne
SURINAM
FRENCH GUIANA
Orinoco
HIGHLANDS
Branco

N
W E
S

Pico da Neblina 3014 m
Negro
Macapá
Marajó Bay
Marajó I.
São Marcos Bay
Belém
São Luís
Japurá
Amazon
Manaus
Santarém
Tocantins
Teresina
Fortaleza
S E L V A S
Madeira
Tapajós
Xingu
Natal
SERTÃO
Recife
Juruá
Purus
Araguaia
São Francisco
Maceió
Rio Branco
Jiparaná
Aripuanã
BRAZIL
Parnaíba
PERU
SERRA DOS PARECIS
Guaporé
Aripuanã
Sobradinho Reservoir
Salvador
BOLIVIA
MATO GROSSO PLATEAU
Cuiabá
Brasília
Goiânia
B R A Z I L I A N HIGHLANDS
Campo Grande
Uberlândia
Belo Horizonte
PARAGUAY
Paraná
Campos
São Paulo
Rio de Janeiro Cape Frio
Itaipu Res.
Santos
Iguaçu Falls
Curitiba
ARGENTINA
Uruguay
Florianópolis
SERRA DO MAR
URUGUAY
Santa Maria
Porto Alegre
Patos Lagoon
Mirim Lake

▼ Flesh-eaters
Shoals of hungry piranha are found in the Amazon basin.

▲ Giant snake
The anaconda can grow to 29.5 feet. It hunts in rivers and pools, strangling or drowning its prey.

▶ Tapir
This rhinoceros-like mammal lives in the tropical rainforests.

▶ In eastern Brazil
This sandstone pillar at Vila Velha, in Brazil's Espírito Sánto state, has been weathered by wind and rain from the South Atlantic.

Brazil and its neighbors

THE NORTHERN HALF OF SOUTH AMERICA IS DIVIDED UP INTO FOUR independent republics. These include Brazil, the largest country in the continent, Venezuela and two small Caribbean countries, Surinam and Guyana. Neighboring French Guiana is still governed directly as a region of France.

This part of the world has huge cities and busy ports as well as remote forest and mountain areas that have never been properly explored. The region has great natural wealth in the form of Venezuelan oil, coal, iron ore, bauxite (for making aluminum), chrome, copper, gold and silver. Brazilian factories make cars and computers.

The rainforests of the Amazon provide timber, but rapid clearance of the forests by farmers, miners and loggers threatens to be a disaster not just for Brazil but for our planet as a whole. Beef cattle are raised on much of the land that has been cleared. Cattle are also reared on the Llanos grasslands of Venezuela.

▲ **Lake of oil**
The Venezuelan economy depends on Lake Maracaibo's oil reserves.

▲ **Pet parrot**
Many parrots are collected from the rainforest to be sold as pets.

▼ **A safe road**
Cattle are herded along the Transpantaneira, the only route through Brazil's Pantanal wetlands.

▼ **Space age**
The rocket launch site at Kourou in French Guiana is operated by the European Space Agency.

▼ **Paramaribo, Surinam**
Paramaribo, at the mouth of the Surinam River, is Surinam's capital and its biggest port. Nearly 50 percent of the population live there.

FACTS

VENEZUELA
República de Venezuela
Area: 352,143 sq miles
Population: 22.3 million
Capital: Caracas
Other cities: Maracaibo, Valencia
Highest point: Pico Bolívar
(16,411 ft)
Official language: Spanish
Currency: bolívar

FRENCH GUIANA
Guyane Française
Overseas region of France
Area: 34,749 sq miles
Population: 0.2 million
Capital: Cayenne
Official language: French
Currency: French franc

◀ Sugarcane
Workers harvest the sugarcane crop. Next, the stalks are crushed and soaked in water to produce a sugary liquid. When this is heated, it separates into brown crystals of cane sugar and sticky molasses.

▼ Cayenne pepper
This hot spice takes its name from the capital of French Guiana.

Brazil is the world's leading producer of coffee and sugarcane. Other crops include rice, maize, soya beans, cassava and citrus fruits. Cayenne, in French Guiana, is famous for its red hot pepper, while Guyana is known for the brown sugar first produced in the Demerara region.

Despite its resources, the region has faced huge economic problems. There has been severe inflation, rising debt and political corruption. Venezuela relies heavily on its oil, for which the price has fallen in recent years.

▼ Brazil nuts

Although some people are wealthy, many are desperately poor. In big cities, such as Caracas or Rio de Janeiro, families with little chance of finding work crowd into makeshift shanty towns and slums. Many of the indigenous peoples of remote areas, referred to as 'Indians', have been killed and had their land stolen. Their rivers have been poisoned and the forests where they hunt have been cut down.

▼ Cassava plantation
The fleshy roots of the cassava plant are used to make flour; its leaves are eaten as a vegetable.

▶ A vanishing world
The Amazon basin contains one-third of the world's surviving rainforest. This is one of the planet's most precious resources, but vast areas have already been destroyed.

Brazil and its neighbors

THE FIRST OR INDIGENOUS PEOPLES OF northern South America now make up only a very small portion of the population. It varies from five percent in Guyana to under two percent in Brazil. They mostly live in scattered communities, many in remote areas of rainforest where they hunt and fish. Groups include the Xingu, Yanomami, Shavanti and Kayapo, the coastal Caribs, Warrau and many others besides. Over 85 indigenous groups have been destroyed over the last 100 years.

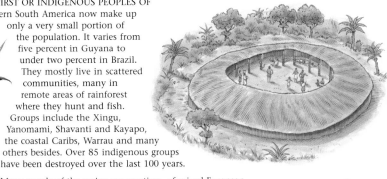

Many people of the region are mestizos, of mixed European and indigenous descent. European settlement of the region has been from Portugal, Spain, Italy, the Netherlands, France, Britain and Germany. There are also sizeable black populations, of African descent. The Caribbean coast has a large Asian population, with many Javanese living in Surinam.

▲ **A rainforest village**
The round huts of the Yanomami may be seen in Venezuela and Brazil. Yanomami lands have been destroyed by mining since the 1970s.

▲ **Kayapo musician**
The Kayapo people live in northeastern Brazil, between the Araguaia and Xingu rivers.

▶ **Java comes to Surinam**
Many workers from Dutch colonies in Southeast Asia found work in Surinam after 1863. They brought their own culture, such as this ritual horse dance.

▲ **On the beach**
Swimmers and sunbathers are attracted to Rio de Janeiro's beaches, on the South Atlantic coast. This one is at a wealthy southern suburb, Barra de Tijuca.

◀ **River borders**
The Paraguay River flows past Corumba, a town on Brazil's frontier with Bolivia. The river goes on to form the Brazil-Paraguay, and Paraguay-Argentina borders.

▲ **Mixed descent**
Brazil is a multiracial society, with many people of mixed indigenous, European or African descent.

◄ **Caracas**
The Venezuelan capital, Caracas, has spread out from its old colonial center to include city parks, high-rise offices and apartments, shopping malls and factories.

▶ **Shanty town**
São Paolo, home to over 15 million people, is Brazil's biggest city. Many desperately poor families live in makeshift housing and slums.

The region's official languages all date from its period of colonial rule – Portuguese in Brazil, Spanish in Venezuela, English in Guyana, Dutch in Surinam and French in French Guiana.

Brazil and Venezuela are largely Roman Catholic, but there are also Protestants and people of other faiths such as Hinduism and Islam. Spirit religions such as Candomblé, influenced by both African and Roman Catholic traditions, are popular in Brazil.

The fascinating mixture of cultures in the region has influenced festivals such as the five-day carnival in Rio de Janeiro, with its dazzling costume parades and dancing to Brazil's very own rhythm, the samba. Ethnic variety has also contributed to regional cooking, which combines African, Asian and European influences.

As in most Latin American regions, soccer is by far the most popular sport. It is practised on almost every beach, village clearing or street corner. Brazil has the most successful World Cup record of any nation.

▼ **Carnival in Rio**
For five days each year the Brazilian city of Rio de Janeiro is taken over by carnival, with costumed revellers dancing the samba in the streets.

▲ **Soccer fans**
Soccer is popular all over South America, and nowhere more so than Brazil, where the national team has won the World Cup four times.

Brazil and its neighbors

THE EARLY PEOPLES OF THE RAINFOREST LEFT BEHIND fewer reminders of their way of life than the peoples of the high Andes. They built with wood, creepers and straw instead of stone – materials which do not survive long in humid, tropical climates. Even so, archaeologists are only now beginning to realise the skill with which these peoples managed the forest, planting trees and seeds they could use for food, medicines and shelter.

▲ **Forest vines**
The forest provided building materials, foods and medicines to the first Amazonians.

The Spanish arrived in Venezuela in 1498, and the Portuguese in Brazil just two years later. Their arrival was a disaster for the indigenous peoples, many of whom died of European diseases. The French and Dutch occupied territory on the Caribbean coast during the 1600s and 1700s, with Britain capturing what is now Guyana in 1796. The Europeans planted sugar cane and other crops, and brought in slave labor from Africa to work on the plantations. Later, many Asian laborers were hired to work along the Caribbean coast.

▲ **Spanish Caracas**
Colonial buildings date back to the days when Venezuela was ruled by Spain.

▼ **Monte Serrat fort**
Several old forts may still be seen in Salvador, this Brazilian port was founded by the Portuguese in 1549.

▲ **Pedro Alvares Cabral**
This Portuguese navigator discovered Brazil by mistake, in 1500. His fleet, bound for India, was carried west by ocean currents.

▶ **Georgetown, Guyana**
The Caribbean port of Georgetown is Guyana's capital. City Hall, on the Avenue of the Republic, dates from the colonial period (1831–1970).

The liberator

Simón Bolívar was born in Venezuela in 1783. In the 1820s, his armies helped to drive the Spanish out of South America.

Opera House, Manaus

Manaus lies in the rainforest, on the Río Negro. Its ornate opera house dates from 1896, when the region was profiting from the rubber trade.

Brasilia

This purpose-built city, planned by architect Lucio Costa, became Brazil's capital in 1960. It was more centrally located than the previous capital, Río de Janeiro.

Venezuela broke away from Spanish rule between 1811 and 1821, after a war of independence led by freedom-fighter Simón Bolívar. Portugal became a kingdom in its own right in 1815 and was declared an independent empire seven years later. However the rich landowners threw out the royal family when it ordered an end to slavery. In 1889, Brazil became a republic. In the 1960s it moved its capital from Rio de Janeiro, on the Atlantic coast, to Brasília, a new, specially-built capital in the center of the country on the Brazilian Highlands.

In 1946 French Guiana, until then chiefly famous for harsh prison settlements such as Devil's Island, became ruled on an equal status with mainland France. Guyana gained independence from Britain in 1970 and Surinam from the Netherlands in 1975.

The oil president

Carlos Andréas Perez was president of Venezuela 1974–9, during the country's oil boom.

Landless protest

Despite Brazil's vast natural resources, many millions of its citizens live below the poverty line. Here, landless farm-laborers join a protest rally in São Paulo.

AD	TIMELINE
400	Marajoara culture, mouth of Amazon
1498	Spanish land in Venezuela
1500	Portuguese claim Brazil
1530	Portuguese colonize Brazil
1593	Spanish claim Surinam
1600s	Sugar plantations in Brazil: slave labor imported from Africa
1602	Dutch settle Surinam
1604	French settle Cayenne
1620s	Dutch settle Guyana
1667	Surinam becomes a Dutch colony
1749	Venezuelan revolt against Spain
1815	Brazil united with Portuguese kingdom
1821	Venezuela joins independent Colombia
1822	Brazil declares independence under Spanish prince, Pedro
1825	Pedro I recognised as emperor of Brazil
1829	Venezuela becomes independent state
1831	Guyana becomes colony of British Guiana
1834	Slavery abolished in British Guiana
1888	Slavery abolished in Brazil
1889	Brazil becomes a republic
1910	Oil discovered in Venezuela
1946	French Guiana becomes overseas department of France
1960	Brasilia becomes capital of Brazil
1966	Guyana becomes independent
1975	Surinam becomes independent
1992	First Earth Summit (UN world environment conference), Río de Janeiro

Argentina and its neighbors

▲ Elephant seals

P araguay lies at the heart of South America. It is crossed by the Paraguay River, which flows into the Paraná. In the west is the tropical wilderness of the Gran Chaco, and in the east both forest and grasslands, taken up by farms and ranches. Uruguay lies on the mouth of the river Plate, on the South Atlantic coast. It is a land of fertile plains and low hills.

In the northeast of Argentina is the rich farmland of the Mesopotamia region, lying between the Paraná and Uruguay rivers. The central north takes in part of the Gran Chaco, while the central eastern region is made up of open, rolling grassland. Known as the pampa, it is now used for ranching and agriculture. To the south again are the bleak, grassy plateaus and valleys of Patagonia.

▲ **In Patagonia**
South of the Río Negro, Argentina is a land of wind-swept plateaus and valleys.

The southern Andes form the border between Argentina and Chile, rising to the highest peaks in all the Americas. Chile lies between the western slopes and the South Pacific Ocean. This narrow coastal strip includes cool green regions, warm lands with a mild, Mediterranean climate, and the Atacama Desert, one of the driest spots on Earth.

▲ **Atacama**
This coastal region of northern Chile is dry, barren desert. However it does contain valuable mineral resources.

Across the Strait of Magellan, the continent breaks up into the islands of Tierra del Fuego and the cold, grey seas off Cape Horn.

▶ **Tierra del Fuego**
The southern tip of South America is a bleak peninsula occupied by both Argentina and Chile. The southernmost town in the world, Ushuaia, lies on the Beagle Channel.

FACTS

ARGENTINA
República Argentina
Area: 1,073,512 sq miles
Population: 35.2 million
Capital: Buenos Aires
Other cities: Córdoba, La Plata, San Miguel de Tucumán
Highest point: Aconcagua (22,831 ft)
Official language: Spanish
Currency: Argentinean peso

CHILE
República de Chile
Area: 292,133 sq miles
Population: 14.4 million
Capital: Santiago
Other cities: Vina del Mar, Valparaíso, Concepción
Highest point: Ojos del Salado (22,572 ft)
Official language: Spanish
Currency: Chilean peso

PARAGUAY
República del Paraguay
Area: 157,047 sq miles
Population: 5.0 million
Capital: Asunción
Other cities: Ciudad del Este, Pedro Juan Caballero
Highest point: Villarrica (2,231 ft)
Official language: Spanish
Currency: guaraní

URUGUAY
República Oriental del Uruguay
Area: 68,500 sq miles
Population: 3.2 million
Capital: Montevideo
Other cities: Salto, Rivera
Highest point: Mirador Nacional (1,644 ft)
Official language: Spanish
Currency: Uruguayan peso

FALKLAND ISLANDS
Islas Malvinas
British Overseas Colony
Area: 4,700 sq miles
Population: 2,000
Capital: Stanley
Official language: English
Currency: Falkland Islands pound

▶ **Canyon lands**
Rivers have carved out canyons from the rocks of Patagonia. The Andes Mountains shield this vast, dry region of Argentina from the Pacific Ocean's rain-bearing winds.

▲ **In the southern Andes**
The heavy ice of the Moreno Glacier grinds its way down to Lago Argentina, one of the most awesome sights in South America.

▼ **Guano rocks**
This rock, near Constitución in central Chile, is covered in guanos (the droppings of seabirds). In parts of South America, guano is a valuable resource. It is collected to make fertilizers.

PARAGUAY

▲ **Prickly pear**

URUGUAY

▲ **Armadillo**

ARGENTINA

N
W   E
S

CHILE

▲ **Curtain of spray**
Argentina borders Brazil along the Iguazú (Iguaçu) River. A long stretch of the river is broken by islands, rapids and waterfalls.

SOUTH GEORGIA (U.K.)

◀ **Volcano**
Volcanic peaks rise above Lake Chungara, in Chile.

▲ **Brown pelican**

55

Map labels:

Arica
Iquique
ATACAMA DESERT
BOLIVIA
Calama
Antofagasta
Ojos del Salado 6,880 m
Copiapó
San Miguel de Tucumán
Santiago del Estero
Catamarca
La Rioja
Coquimbo
Pta. Lengua de Vaca
Aconcagua 6,959 m
Valparaíso
Santiago
Rancagua
San Juan
Mendoza
San Luis
San Rafael
Talca
Chillán
Concepción
Pta. Lavapié
Valdivia
Pta. de la Galera
Osorno
Puerto Montt
Chiloé I.
C. Quilán
LOS CHONOS ARCHIPELAGO
Lake Buenos Aires
Peñas Gulf
PACIFIC OCEAN
Wellington I.
REINA ADELAIDA ARCHIPELAGO
Santa Inés I.
Salta
Verde
Pilcomayo
Bermejo
Formosa
Resistencia
Corrientes
Parana
Concepción
Asunción
Ciudad del Este
Alto Paraná
Posadas
MESOPOTAMIA
Uruguay
Mar Chiquito
Córdoba
SIERRA DE CÓRDOBA
Concordia
Salto
Paysandu
Santa Fe
Paraná
Rosario
Río Cuarto
Buenos Aires
La Plata
Montevideo
Río de La Plata
Pta. Norte
Cape San Antonio
PAMPAS
Mar del Plata
Cape Corrientes
Bahía Blanca
Colorado
Neuquén
Negro
Viedma
San Matías Gulf
Valdés Peninsula
Rawson
Chubut
Chico
Comodoro Rivadavia
San Jorge Gulf
C. Tres Puntas
Puerto Deseado
Deseado
Chico
Santa Cruz
Puerto Santa Cruz
Bahía Grande
Río Gallegos
Punta Arenas
Tierra del Fuego
Santa Inés I.
C. San Diego
Ushuaia
Cape Horn
Strait of Magellan
FALKLAND/MALVINAS ISLANDS
West Falkland
East Falkland
Stanley
BRAZIL
GRAN CHACO
ANDES MOUNTAINS
PATAGONIA
Negro
Limay
Salado

Argentina and its neighbors

THE SOUTHERN MAINLAND OF SOUTH AMERICA is divided into four independent republics – the small northern nations of Uruguay and Paraguay, the wide open spaces of Argentina and the long, narrow territory of Chile. The region has experienced long years of rule by brutal military regimes and there have also been wars over borders and territory. In 1982 Argentina went to war with the United Kingdom over ownership of the Falkland or Malvinas Islands, a small British colony in the South Atlantic Ocean. Today the region as a whole has moved to democratic systems of government, but faces many economic and political problems.

▲ Atlantic outpost
Sheep are raised on the remote British colony of the Falkland Islands, or Islas Malvinas.

▲ Military rule
The army held power in Argentina from 1976 to 1983, in Chile from 1973 to 1989, in Paraguay from 1954 to 1993, and in Uruguay from 1973 to 1984.

Paraguay raises cattle, and grows cotton. The leaves of a plant called the Paraguay holly are used to make a bitter tea called yerba maté, which is also very popular in Argentina. Uruguay, too, is cattle country, with fruit grown on the coastal plains.

▶ Cattle Market
A Chilean cowboy is called a huaso. Cattle are raised in the the central Chilean regions to the south of Santiago.

▲ Salt lake
The bone-dry air of Chile's Atacama Desert evaporates pools of water, leaving behind salt pans.

▶ Valdés wildlife
Magellan penguins may be seen off Argentina's Valdés peninsula, along with elephant seals and whales.

◀ Yoked oxon
Oxen are yoked in the traditional way on this farm near Coyhaique, in Patagonia.

▶ City memorial
This obelisk rises above the Plaza de la República in central Buenos Aires. It commemorates the founding of the city in 1536.

Itaipú dam
This is the world's biggest hydroelectric scheme, jointly operated by Argentina and Paraguay. Building the dam created a 521 sq miles reservoir, at a cost of US$25 billion.

Argentina first became wealthy by exporting beef. Great herds of cattle are still raised on the pampa, and Patagonia raises sheep. The foothills of the Andes provide shelter for vineyards in the sunny region around Mendoza. Fisheries, oil and natural gas are important industries of the far south – Ushuaia is the most southerly town in the world. Industry is centered around the capital of Buenos Aires and is based on food processing, leather goods, textiles, chemicals and car manufacture.

Chile's industry is based around the port of Valparaiso, where iron, steel, chemicals and textiles are produced, and the capital city of Santiago. The country has large reserves of copper in the north. The warm regions of central Chile produce wine and citrus fruits for export and the long coastline provides harbors for large fishing fleets.

Argentinian wines
The sheltered region around Mendoza has a mild, dry climate. Rivers and irrigation schemes have allowed vines to be grown here since the 1600s.

Plaza del Congreso
At the heart of Buenos Aires, capital of Argentina, is the Palace of Congress. Congress is made up of two houses, the Senate and the Chamber of Deputies.

Juicy fruit
The orchards of central Chile produce fruit for export, including oranges, lemons, apples, grapes and pears.

Copper kings
Chile is the world's biggest copper producer. The monster Chuquicamata open-cast mine is sited in the far north, in the Atacama Desert.

Santiago
Nine out of ten Chileans live in towns or cities. The capital is the country's largest city. It is home to nearly five million people.

Argentina and its neighbors

NATIVE AMERICAN PEOPLES MIGRATED SOUTHWARDS through the continent in prehistoric times. They had reached central South America by 14,000BC and were in Patagonia by 12,000BC. While northern Chile came under the influence of the great civilizations of the northern Andes, the peoples of the far south lived by hunting on the grasslands or fishing the cold southern waters in their canoes.

▲ **Araucarian people**
The indigenous Araucanians of Chile include the Mapuche, who resisted conquest for over 300 years.

The Spanish invaded the region in the 1500s. They were fiercely resisted by indigenous groups such as the Querandí of the pampa and the Mapuche of Chile. The region broke away from Spanish rule in the 1800s, but generals and warlords fought out regional and civil wars. There was also genocide, the organized murder of whole native peoples. The pampa of Argentina were taken over by huge ranches. They were worked by gauchos, wild-living cowboys of mixed Spanish-indigenous descent.

Immigrants poured into the region in the 1800s and 1900s – Spanish, Italians, Basques, Welsh, English, Germans, Swiss, Poles, Russians, Jews, Syrians. More recently there were arrivals from Japan, Korea and from other parts of South America.

▲ **Desert mummy**
Dead bodies from early South American civilizations have been preserved as mummies. This woman was found in the Atacama Desert.

▼ **The gauchos**
The tough, bragging cowboys of the Argentinean pampas were called gauchos. Today's cowboys still honor the gaucho tradition.

▼ **La Boca**
This district of Buenos Aires, along the polluted Riachuelo waterway, was founded by poor Basque and Italian immigrants. Today it is a center for artists, and the buildings are painted in bold, bright colors.

▲ **Andean church**
A white church stands on the edge of the Andes at Tocanao, in Chile's Antofagasta region. It is built from volcanic stone.

▼ Polo champions
Eduardo Heguy comes from a family of polo stars. Argentina has achieved international success in this exclusive sport.

▶ Armadillo lute
The shell of the armadillo is used to make a traditional stringed instrument.

▶ Eva Perón (1919–52)
This former actress married Argentinean politician Juan Perón in 1945. 'Evita' was a popular and powerful influence on the country.

Today the descendants of all these peoples dominate the region. Indigenous peoples now make up a tiny percentage of the population, but their cultures survive in some areas. The native Guaraní language is widely spoken in Paraguay. Spanish is spoken everywhere, but other European languages, from Italian to Welsh, may also be heard. Far out in the South Atlantic, the Falkland Islanders remain English in their speech and customs. The mainland nations are mostly Roman Catholic, with Protestant and Jewish minorities.

The region has produced sporting champions in motor racing, soccer and tennis, and the Andes Mountains are increasingly popular for skiing and outdoor pursuits. Both Chile and Argentina have produced great writers and poets in the last century, including the Argentinian Jorge Luis Borges (1899–1986) and the Chilean novelist Isabel Allende (b.1942).

▲ Viña del Mar
South American tourists flock to this resort, near Valparaíso in Chile, for the beaches and casino.

▶ Grand Prix
Motor racing has been a passion since the 1950s, when Argentinian Juan Fangio was five times Grand Prix champion.

AD	TIMELINE
1516	*Río de la Plata discovered by the Spanish*
1536	*First founding of Buenos Aires by Spanish*
1537	*Spanish found Asunción*
1541	*Querandí people attack Buenos Aires*
	Spanish conquer Chile
1543	*Rebuilding Buenos Aires (until 1580)*
1726	*Spanish build fort at Montevideo*
1811	*Paraguay becomes independent*
1816	*Argentina becomes independent*
1818	*Chile becomes independent*
1825	*Uruguay declares independence (recognized 1828)*
1857	*European settlement of the pampa*
1865	*Paraguay fights Uruguay, Argentina and Brazil (until 1870)*
1878	*Wars against Native Americans in Argentina (until 1883)*
1879	*War of the Pacific (until 1884): Chile defeats Peru and Bolivia*
1946	*Juan Perón becomes Argentinean president*
1954	*Military coup in Paraguay*
1973	*Allende overthrown by General Augusto Pinochet in Chile*
1976	*Military rule in Argentina: imprisonment and murder of opponents*
1982	*Argentina fights United Kingdom over the Falkland (Malvinas) Islands*
1983	*Democracy restored in Argentina*
1992	*Democracy restored in Paraguay*

INDEX

Joel Segovia

Joel Segovia

Joel Segovia